VIII. *A Dynamical Theory of the Electromagnetic Field.* By J. Clerk Maxwell, *F.R.S.*

Received October 27,—Read December 8, 1864.

PART I.—INTRODUCTORY.

(1) The most obvious mechanical phenomenon in electrical and magnetical experiments is the mutual action by which bodies in certain states set each other in motion while still at a sensible distance from each other. The first step, therefore, in reducing these phenomena into scientific form, is to ascertain the magnitude and direction of the force acting between the bodies, and when it is found that this force depends in a certain way upon the relative position of the bodies and on their electric or magnetic condition, it seems at first sight natural to explain the facts by assuming the existence of something either at rest or in motion in each body, constituting its electric or magnetic state, and capable of acting at a distance according to mathematical laws.

In this way mathematical theories of statical electricity, of magnetism, of the mechanical action between conductors carrying currents, and of the induction of currents have been formed. In these theories the force acting between the two bodies is treated with reference only to the condition of the bodies and their relative position, and without any express consideration of the surrounding medium.

These theories assume, more or less explicitly, the existence of substances the particles of which have the property of acting on one another at a distance by attraction or repulsion. The most complete development of a theory of this kind is that of M. W. Weber*, who has made the same theory include electrostatic and electromagnetic phenomena.

In doing so, however, he has found it necessary to assume that the force between two electric particles depends on their relative velocity, as well as on their distance.

This theory, as developed by MM. W. Weber and C. Neumann†, is exceedingly ingenious, and wonderfully comprehensive in its application to the phenomena of statical electricity, electromagnetic attractions, induction of currents and diamagnetic phenomena; and it comes to us with the more authority, as it has served to guide the speculations of one who has made so great an advance in the practical part of electric science, both by introducing a consistent system of units in electrical measurement, and by actually determining electrical quantities with an accuracy hitherto unknown.

* Electrodynamische Maassbestimmungen. Leipzic Trans. vol. i. 1849, and Taylor's Scientific Memoirs, vol. v. art. xiv.

† "Explicare tentatur quomodo fiat ut lucis planum polarizationis per vires electricas vel magneticas declinetur."—Halis Saxonum, 1858.

(2) The mechanical difficulties, however, which are involved in the assumption of particles acting at a distance with forces which depend on their velocities are such as to prevent me from considering this theory as an ultimate one, though it may have been, and may yet be useful in leading to the coordination of phenomena.

I have therefore preferred to seek an explanation of the fact in another direction, by supposing them to be produced by actions which go on in the surrounding medium as well as in the excited bodies, and endeavouring to explain the action between distant bodies without assuming the existence of forces capable of acting directly at sensible distances.

(3) The theory I propose may therefore be called a theory of the *Electromagnetic Field,* because it has to do with the space in the neighbourhood of the electric or magnetic bodies, and it may be called a *Dynamical* Theory, because it assumes that in that space there is matter in motion, by which the observed electromagnetic phenomena are produced.

(4) The electromagnetic field is that part of space which contains and surrounds bodies in electric or magnetic conditions.

It may be filled with any kind of matter, or we may endeavour to render it empty of all gross matter, as in the case of GEISSLER'S tubes and other so-called vacua.

There is always, however, enough of matter left to receive and transmit the undulations of light and heat, and it is because the transmission of these radiations is not greatly altered when transparent bodies of measurable density are substituted for the so-called vacuum, that we are obliged to admit that the undulations are those of an æthereal substance, and not of the gross matter, the presence of which merely modifies in some way the motion of the æther.

We have therefore some reason to believe, from the phenomena of light and heat, that there is an æthereal medium filling space and permeating bodies, capable of being set in motion and of transmitting that motion from one part to another, and of communicating that motion to gross matter so as to heat it and affect it in various ways.

(5) Now the energy communicated to the body in heating it must have formerly existed in the moving medium, for the undulations had left the source of heat some time before they reached the body, and during that time the energy must have been half in the form of motion of the medium and half in the form of elastic resilience. From these considerations Professor W. THOMSON has argued*, that the medium must have a density capable of comparison with that of gross matter, and has even assigned an inferior limit to that density.

(6) We may therefore receive, as a datum derived from a branch of science independent of that with which we have to deal, the existence of a pervading medium, of small but real density, capable of being set in motion, and of transmitting motion from one part to another with great, but not infinite, velocity.

Hence the parts of this medium must be so connected that the motion of one part

---

* "On the Possible Density of the Luminiferous Medium, and on the Mechanical Value of a Cubic Mile of Sunlight," Transactions of the Royal Society of Edinburgh (1854), p. 57.

DS\

depends in some way on the motion of the rest; and at the same time these connexions must be capable of a certain kind of elastic yielding, since the communication of motion is not instantaneous, but occupies time.

The medium is therefore capable of receiving and storing up two kinds of energy, namely, the "actual" energy depending on the motions of its parts, and "potential" energy, consisting of the work which the medium will do in recovering from displacement in virtue of its elasticity.

The propagation of undulations consists in the continual transformation of one of these forms of energy into the other alternately, and at any instant the amount of energy in the whole medium is equally divided, so that half is energy of motion, and half is elastic resilience.

(7) A medium having such a constitution may be capable of other kinds of motion and displacement than those which produce the phenomena of light and heat, and some of these may be of such a kind that they may be evidenced to our senses by the phenomena they produce.

(8) Now we know that the luminiferous medium is in certain cases acted on by magnetism; for FARADAY* discovered that when a plane polarized ray traverses a transparent diamagnetic medium in the direction of the lines of magnetic force produced by magnets or currents in the neighbourhood, the plane of polarization is caused to rotate.

This rotation is always in the direction in which positive electricity must be carried round the diamagnetic body in order to produce the actual magnetization of the field.

M. VERDET† has since discovered that if a paramagnetic body, such as solution of perchloride of iron in ether, be substituted for the diamagnetic body, the rotation is in the opposite direction.

Now Professor W. THOMSON‡ has pointed out that no distribution of forces acting between the parts of a medium whose only motion is that of the luminous vibrations, is sufficient to account for the phenomena, but that we must admit the existence of a motion in the medium depending on the magnetization, in addition to the vibratory motion which constitutes light.

It is true that the rotation by magnetism of the plane of polarization has been observed only in media of considerable density; but the properties of the magnetic field are not so much altered by the substitution of one medium for another, or for a vacuum, as to allow us to suppose that the dense medium does anything more than merely modify the motion of the ether. We have therefore warrantable grounds for inquiring whether there may not be a motion of the ethereal medium going on wherever magnetic effects are observed, and we have some reason to suppose that this motion is one of rotation, having the direction of the magnetic force as its axis.

(9) We may now consider another phenomenon observed in the electromagnetic

* Experimental Researches, Series 19.
† Comptes Rendus (1856, second half year, p. 529, and 1857, first half year, p. 1209).
‡ Proceedings of the Royal Society, June 1856 and June 1861.

field. When a body is moved across the lines of magnetic force it experiences what is called an electromotive force; the two extremities of the body tend to become oppositely electrified, and an electric current tends to flow through the body. When the electromotive force is sufficiently powerful, and is made to act on certain compound bodies, it decomposes them, and causes one of their components to pass towards one extremity of the body, and the other in the opposite direction.

Here we have evidence of a force causing an electric current in spite of resistance; electrifying the extremities of a body in opposite ways, a condition which is sustained only by the action of the electromotive force, and which, as soon as that force is removed, tends, with an equal and opposite force, to produce a counter current through the body and to restore the original electrical state of the body; and finally, if strong enough, tearing to pieces chemical compounds and carrying their components in opposite directions, while their natural tendency is to combine, and to combine with a force which can generate an electromotive force in the reverse direction.

This, then, is a force acting on a body caused by its motion through the electromagnetic field, or by changes occurring in that field itself; and the effect of the force is either to produce a current and heat the body, or to decompose the body, or, when it can do neither, to put the body in a state of electric polarization,—a state of constraint in which opposite extremities are oppositely electrified, and from which the body tends to relieve itself as soon as the disturbing force is removed.

(10) According to the theory which I propose to explain, this "electromotive force" is the force called into play during the communication of motion from one part of the medium to another, and it is by means of this force that the motion of one part causes motion in another part. When electromotive force acts on a conducting circuit, it produces a current, which, as it meets with resistance, occasions a continual transformation of electrical energy into heat, which is incapable of being restored again to the form of electrical energy by any reversal of the process.

(11) But when electromotive force acts on a dielectric it produces a state of polarization of its parts similar in distribution to the polarity of the parts of a mass of iron under the influence of a magnet, and like the magnetic polarization, capable of being described as a state in which every particle has its opposite poles in opposite conditions*.

In a dielectric under the action of electromotive force, we may conceive that the electricity in each molecule is so displaced that one side is rendered positively and the other negatively electrical, but that the electricity remains entirely connected with the molecule, and does not pass from one molecule to another. The effect of this action on the whole dielectric mass is to produce a general displacement of electricity in a certain direction. This displacement does not amount to a current, because when it has attained to a certain value it remains constant, but it is the commencement of a current, and its variations constitute currents in the positive or the negative direction according

* FARADAY, Exp. Res. Series XI.; MOSSOTTI, Mem. della Soc. Italiana (Modena), vol. xxiv. part 2. p. 49.

as the displacement is increasing or decreasing. In the interior of the dielectric there is no indication of electrification, because the electrification of the surface of any molecule is neutralized by the opposite electrification of the surface of the molecules in contact with it; but at the bounding surface of the dielectric, where the electrification is not neutralized, we find the phenomena which indicate positive or negative electrification.

The relation between the electromotive force and the amount of electric displacement it produces depends on the nature of the dielectric, the same electromotive force producing generally a greater electric displacement in solid dielectrics, such as glass or sulphur, than in air.

(12) Here, then, we perceive another effect of electromotive force, namely, electric displacement, which according to our theory is a kind of elastic yielding to the action of the force, similar to that which takes place in structures and machines owing to the want of perfect rigidity of the connexions.

(13) The practical investigation of the inductive capacity of dielectrics is rendered difficult on account of two disturbing phenomena. The first is the conductivity of the dielectric, which, though in many cases exceedingly small, is not altogether insensible. The second is the phenomenon called electric absorption*, in virtue of which, when the dielectric is exposed to electromotive force, the electric displacement gradually increases, and when the electromotive force is removed, the dielectric does not instantly return to its primitive state, but only discharges a portion of its electrification, and when left to itself gradually acquires electrification on its surface, as the interior gradually becomes depolarized. Almost all solid dielectrics exhibit this phenomenon, which gives rise to the residual charge in the Leyden jar, and to several phenomena of electric cables described by Mr. F. JENKIN †.

(14) We have here two other kinds of yielding besides the yielding of the perfect dielectric, which we have compared to a perfectly elastic body. The yielding due to conductivity may be compared to that of a viscous fluid (that is to say, a fluid having great internal friction), or a soft solid on which the smallest force produces a permanent alteration of figure increasing with the time during which the force acts. The yielding due to electric absorption may be compared to that of a cellular elastic body containing a thick fluid in its cavities. Such a body, when subjected to pressure, is compressed by degrees on account of the gradual yielding of the thick fluid; and when the pressure is removed it does not at once recover its figure, because the elasticity of the substance of the body has gradually to overcome the tenacity of the fluid before it can regain complete equilibrium.

Several solid bodies in which no such structure as we have supposed can be found, seem to possess a mechanical property of this kind ‡; and it seems probable that the

* FARADAY, Exp. Res. 1233–1250.

† Reports of British Association, 1859, p. 248; and Report of Committee of Board of Trade on Submarine Cables, pp. 136 & 464.

‡ As, for instance, the composition of glue, treacle, &c., of which small plastic figures are made, which after being distorted gradually recover their shape.

same substances, if dielectrics, may possess the analogous electrical property, and if magnetic, may have corresponding properties relating to the acquisition, retention, and loss of magnetic polarity.

(15) It appears therefore that certain phenomena in electricity and magnetism lead to the same conclusion as those of optics, namely, that there is an æthereal medium pervading all bodies, and modified only in degree by their presence; that the parts of this medium are capable of being set in motion by electric currents and magnets; that this motion is communicated from one part of the medium to another by forces arising from the connexions of those parts; that under the action of these forces there is a certain yielding depending on the elasticity of these connexions; and that therefore energy in two different forms may exist in the medium, the one form being the actual energy of motion of its parts, and the other being the potential energy stored up in the connexions, in virtue of their elasticity.

(16) Thus, then, we are led to the conception of a complicated mechanism capable of a vast variety of motion, but at the same time so connected that the motion of one part depends, according to definite relations, on the motion of other parts, these motions being communicated by forces arising from the relative displacement of the connected parts, in virtue of their elasticity. Such a mechanism must be subject to the general laws of Dynamics, and we ought to be able to work out all the consequences of its motion, provided we know the form of the relation between the motions of the parts.

(17) We know that when an electric current is established in a conducting circuit, the neighbouring part of the field is characterized by certain magnetic properties, and that if two circuits are in the field, the magnetic properties of the field due to the two currents are combined. Thus each part of the field is in connexion with both currents, and the two currents are put in connexion with each other in virtue of their connexion with the magnetization of the field. The first result of this connexion that I propose to examine, is the induction of one current by another, and by the motion of conductors in the field.

The second result, which is deduced from this, is the mechanical action between conductors carrying currents. The phenomenon of the induction of currents has been deduced from their mechanical action by HELMHOLTZ[*] and THOMSON[†]. I have followed the reverse order, and deduced the mechanical action from the laws of induction. I have then described experimental methods of determining the quantities L, M, N, on which these phenomena depend.

(18) I then apply the phenomena of induction and attraction of currents to the exploration of the electromagnetic field, and the laying down systems of lines of magnetic force which indicate its magnetic properties. By exploring the same field with a magnet, I show the distribution of its equipotential magnetic surfaces, cutting the lines of force at right angles.

* "Conservation of Force," Physical Society of Berlin, 1847; and TAYLOR's Scientific Memoirs, 1853, p. 114.

† Reports of the British Association, 1848; Philosophical Magazine, Dec. 1851.

In order to bring these results within the power of symbolical calculation, I then express them in the form of the General Equations of the Electromagnetic Field. These equations express—

- (A) The relation between electric displacement, true conduction, and the total current, compounded of both.
- (B) The relation between the lines of magnetic force and the inductive coefficients of a circuit, as already deduced from the laws of induction.
- (C) The relation between the strength of a current and its magnetic effects, according to the electromagnetic system of measurement.
- (D) The value of the electromotive force in a body, as arising from the motion of the body in the field, the alteration of the field itself, and the variation of electric potential from one part of the field to another.
- (E) The relation between electric displacement, and the electromotive force which produces it.
- (F) The relation between an electric current, and the electromotive force which produces it.
- (G) The relation between the amount of free electricity at any point, and the electric displacements in the neighbourhood.
- (H) The relation between the increase or diminution of free electricity and the electric currents in the neighbourhood.

There are twenty of these equations in all, involving twenty variable quantities.

(19) I then express in terms of these quantities the intrinsic energy of the Electromagnetic Field as depending partly on its magnetic and partly on its electric polarization at every point.

From this I determine the mechanical force acting, 1st, on a moveable conductor carrying an electric current; 2ndly, on a magnetic pole; 3rdly, on an electrified body.

The last result, namely, the mechanical force acting on an electrified body, gives rise to an independent method of electrical measurement founded on its electrostatic effects. The relation between the units employed in the two methods is shown to depend on what I have called the "electric elasticity" of the medium, and to be a velocity, which has been experimentally determined by MM. WEBER and KOHLRAUSCH.

I then show how to calculate the electrostatic capacity of a condenser, and the specific inductive capacity of a dielectric.

The case of a condenser composed of parallel layers of substances of different electric resistances and inductive capacities is next examined, and it is shown that the phenomenon called electric absorption will generally occur, that is, the condenser, when suddenly discharged, will after a short time show signs of a *residual* charge.

(20) The general equations are next applied to the case of a magnetic disturbance propagated through a non-conducting field, and it is shown that the only disturbances which can be so propagated are those which are transverse to the direction of propagation, and that the velocity of propagation is the velocity v, found from experiments such

as those of WEBER, which expresses the number of electrostatic units of electricity which are contained in one electromagnetic unit.

This velocity is so nearly that of light, that it seems we have strong reason to conclude that light itself (including radiant heat, and other radiations if any) is an electromagnetic disturbance in the form of waves propagated through the electromagnetic field according to electromagnetic laws. If so, the agreement between the elasticity of the medium as calculated from the rapid alternations of luminous vibrations, and as found by the slow processes of electrical experiments, shows how perfect and regular the elastic properties of the medium must be when not encumbered with any matter denser than air. If the same character of the elasticity is retained in dense transparent bodies, it appears that the square of the index of refraction is equal to the product of the specific dielectric capacity and the specific magnetic capacity. Conducting media are shown to absorb such radiations rapidly, and therefore to be generally opaque.

The conception of the propagation of transverse magnetic disturbances to the exclusion of normal ones is distinctly set forth by Professor FARADAY* in his "Thoughts on Ray Vibrations." The electromagnetic theory of light, as proposed by him, is the same in substance as that which I have begun to develope in this paper, except that in 1846 there were no data to calculate the velocity of propagation.

(21) The general equations are then applied to the calculation of the coefficients of mutual induction of two circular currents and the coefficient of self-induction in a coil. The want of uniformity of the current in the different parts of the section of a wire at the commencement of the current is investigated, I believe for the first time, and the consequent correction of the coefficient of self-induction is found.

These results are applied to the calculation of the self-induction of the coil used in the experiments of the Committee of the British Association on Standards of Electric Resistance, and the value compared with that deduced from the experiments.

PART II.—ON ELECTROMAGNETIC INDUCTION.

Electromagnetic Momentum of a Current.

(22) We may begin by considering the state of the field in the neighbourhood of an electric current. We know that magnetic forces are excited in the field, their direction and magnitude depending according to known laws upon the form of the conductor carrying the current. When the strength of the current is increased, all the magnetic effects are increased in the same proportion. Now, if the magnetic state of the field depends on motions of the medium, a certain force must be exerted in order to increase or diminish these motions, and when the motions are excited they continue, so that the effect of the connexion between the current and the electromagnetic field surrounding it, is to endow the current with a kind of momentum, just as the connexion between the driving-point of a machine and a fly-wheel endows the driving-point with an addi-

* Philosophical Magazine, May 1846, or Experimental Researches, iii. p. 447.

tional momentum, which may be called the momentum of the fly-wheel reduced to the driving-point. The unbalanced force acting on the driving-point increases this momentum, and is measured by the rate of its increase.

In the case of electric currents, the resistance to sudden increase or diminution of strength produces effects exactly like those of momentum, but the amount of this momentum depends on the shape of the conductor and the relative position of its different parts.

Mutual Action of two Currents.

(23) If there are two electric currents in the field, the magnetic force at any point is that compounded of the forces due to each current separately, and since the two currents are in connexion with every point of the field, they will be in connexion with each other, so that any increase or diminution of the one will produce a force acting with or contrary to the other.

Dynamical Illustration of Reduced Momentum.

(24) As a dynamical illustration, let us suppose a body C so connected with two independent driving-points A and B that its velocity is p times that of A together with q times that of B. Let u be the velocity of A, v that of B, and w that of C, and let δx, δy, δz be their simultaneous displacements, then by the general equation of dynamics[*],

$$C\frac{dw}{dt}\delta z = X\delta x + Y\delta y,$$

where X and Y are the forces acting at A and B.

But

$$\frac{dw}{dt} = p\frac{du}{dt} + q\frac{dv}{dt},$$

and

$$\delta z = p\delta x + q\delta y.$$

Substituting, and remembering that δx and δy are independent,

$$\left.\begin{aligned} X &= \frac{d}{dt}(Cp^2u + Cpqv), \\ Y &= \frac{d}{dt}(Cpqu + Cq^2v). \end{aligned}\right\} \quad \cdots \cdots \cdots \cdots (1)$$

We may call $Cp^2u + Cpqv$ the momentum of C referred to A, and $Cpqu + Cq^2v$ its momentum referred to B; then we may say that the effect of the force X is to increase the momentum of C referred to A, and that of Y to increase its momentum referred to B.

If there are many bodies connected with A and B in a similar way but with different values of p and q, we may treat the question in the same way by assuming

$$L = \Sigma(Cp^2), \quad M = \Sigma(Cpq), \quad \text{and} \quad N = \Sigma(Cq^2),$$

---

[*] LAGRANGE, Méc. Anal. ii. 2. § 5.

where the summation is extended to all the bodies with their proper values of C, p, and q. Then the momentum of the system referred to A is

$$Lu + Mv,$$

and referred to B,

$$Mu + Nv,$$

and we shall have

$$X = \frac{d}{dt}(Lu + Mv),$$
$$Y = \frac{d}{dt}(Mu + Nv),$$

. . . . (2)

where X and Y are the external forces acting on A and B.

(25) To make the illustration more complete we have only to suppose that the motion of A is resisted by a force proportional to its velocity, which we may call Ru, and that of B by a similar force, which we may call Sv, R and S being coefficients of resistance. Then if ξ and η are the forces on A and B

$$\xi = X + Ru = Ru + \frac{d}{dt}(Lu + Mv),$$
$$\eta = Y + Sv = Sv + \frac{d}{dt}(Mu + Nv)$$

. . . . (3)

If the velocity of A be increased at the rate $\frac{du}{dt}$, then in order to prevent B from moving a force, $\eta = \frac{d}{dt}(Mu)$ must be applied to it.

This effect on B, due to an increase of the velocity of A, corresponds to the electromotive force on one circuit arising from an increase in the strength of a neighbouring circuit.

This dynamical illustration is to be considered merely as assisting the reader to understand what is meant in mechanics by Reduced Momentum. The facts of the induction of currents as depending on the variations of the quantity called Electromagnetic Momentum, or Electrotonic State, rest on the experiments of FARADAY[*], FELICI[†], &c.

Coefficients of Induction for Two Circuits.

(26) In the electromagnetic field the values of L, M, N depend on the distribution of the magnetic effects due to the two circuits, and this distribution depends only on the form and relative position of the circuits. Hence L, M, N are quantities depending on the form and relative position of the circuits, and are subject to variation with the motion of the conductors. It will be presently seen that L, M, N are geometrical quantities of the nature of lines, that is, of one dimension in space; L depends on the form of the first conductor, which we shall call A, N on that of the second, which we shall call B, and M on the relative position of A and B.

(27) Let ξ be the electromotive force acting on A, x the strength of the current, and

[*] Experimental Researches, Series I., IX.   [†] Annales de Chimie, sér. 3. xxxiv. (1852) p. 64.

R the resistance, then Rx will be the resisting force. In steady currents the electromotive force just balances the resisting force, but in variable currents the resultant force ξ=Rx is expended in increasing the "electromagnetic momentum," using the word momentum merely to express that which is generated by a force acting during a time, that is, a velocity existing in a body.

In the case of electric currents, the force in action is not ordinary mechanical force, at least we are not as yet able to measure it as common force, but we call it electromotive force, and the body moved is not merely the electricity in the conductor, but something outside the conductor, and capable of being affected by other conductors in the neighbourhood carrying currents. In this it resembles rather the reduced momentum of a driving-point of a machine as influenced by its mechanical connexions, than that of a simple moving body like a cannon ball, or water in a tube.

Electromagnetic Relations of two Conducting Circuits.

(28.) In the case of two conducting circuits, A and B, we shall assume that the electromagnetic momentum belonging to A is

$$L x + M y,$$

and that belonging to B,

$$M x + N y,$$

where L, M, N correspond to the same quantities in the dynamical illustration, except that they are supposed to be capable of variation when the conductors A or B are moved.

Then the equation of the current x in A will be

$$\xi = R x + \frac{d}{dt}(L x + M y), \quad \ldots \quad \ldots \quad \ldots \quad (4)$$

and that of y in B

$$\eta = S y + \frac{d}{dt}(M x + N y), \quad \ldots \quad \ldots \quad \ldots \quad (5)$$

where ξ and η are the electromotive forces, x and y the currents, and R and S the resistances in A and B respectively.

Induction of one Current by another.

(29) Case 1st. Let there be no electromotive force on B, except that which arises from the action of A, and let the current of A increase from 0 to the value x, then

$$S y + \frac{d}{dt}(M x + N y) = 0,$$

whence

$$Y = \int_0^t y \, dt = -\frac{M}{S} x,$$

that is, a quantity of electricity Y, being the total induced current, will flow through B when x rises from 0 to x. This is induction by variation of the current in the primary

3 s 2

conductor. When M is positive, the induced current due to increase of the primary current is negative.

Induction by Motion of Conductor.

(30) Case 2nd. Let x remain constant, and let M change from M to M', then

$$Y = -\frac{M'-M}{S}x;$$

so that, if M is increased, which it will be by the primary and secondary circuits approaching each other, there will be a negative induced current, the total quantity of electricity passed through B being Y.

This is induction by the relative motion of the primary and secondary conductors.

Equation of Work and Energy.

(31) To form the equation between work done and energy produced, multiply (1) by x and (2) by y, and add

$$\xi x + \eta y = Rx^2 + Sy^2 + x\frac{d}{dt}(Lx+My)+y\frac{d}{dt}(Mx+Ny). \quad . \quad . \quad . \quad (8)$$

Here ξx is the work done in unit of time by the electromotive force ξ acting on the current x and maintaining it, and ηy is the work done by the electromotive force η. Hence the left-hand side of the equation represents the work done by the electromotive forces in unit of time.

Heat produced by the Current.

(32) On the other side of the equation we have, first,

$$Rx^2 + Sy^2 = H, \quad . \quad . \quad . \quad . \quad . \quad . \quad . \quad . \quad . \quad . \quad (9)$$

which represents the work done in overcoming the resistance of the circuits in unit of time. This is converted into heat. The remaining terms represent work not converted into heat. They may be written

$$\tfrac{1}{2}\frac{d}{dt}(Lx^2+2Mxy+Ny^2)+\tfrac{1}{2}\frac{dL}{dt}x^2+\frac{dM}{dt}xy+\tfrac{1}{2}\frac{dN}{dt}y^2.$$

Intrinsic Energy of the Currents.

(33) If L, M, N are constant, the whole work of the electromotive forces which is not spent against resistance will be devoted to the development of the currents. The whole intrinsic energy of the currents is therefore

$$\tfrac{1}{2}Lx^2+Mxy+\tfrac{1}{2}Ny^2=E. \quad . \quad . \quad . \quad . \quad . \quad . \quad . \quad (10)$$

This energy exists in a form imperceptible to our senses, probably as actual motion, the seat of this motion being not merely the conducting circuits, but the space surrounding them.

Mechanical Action between Conductors.

(34) The remaining terms,

$$\tfrac{1}{2}\frac{dL}{dt}x^2 + \frac{dM}{dt}xy + \tfrac{1}{2}\frac{dN}{dt}y^2 = W \quad . \quad . \quad . \quad . \quad . \quad . \quad . \quad (11)$$

represent the work done in unit of time arising from the variations of L, M, and N, or, what is the same thing, alterations in the form and position of the conducting circuits A and B.

Now if work is done when a body is moved, it must arise from ordinary mechanical force acting on the body while it is moved. Hence this part of the expression shows that there is a mechanical force urging every part of the conductors themselves in that direction in which L, M, and N will be most increased.

The existence of the electromagnetic force between conductors carrying currents is therefore a direct consequence of the joint and independent action of each current on the electromagnetic field. If A and B are allowed to approach a distance *ds*, so as to increase M from M to M' while the currents are *x* and *y*, then the work done will be

$$(M'-M)xy,$$

and the force in the direction of *ds* will be

$$\frac{dM}{ds}xy, \quad . \quad . \quad . \quad . \quad . \quad . \quad . \quad . \quad . \quad . \quad (12)$$

and this will be an attraction if *x* and *y* are of the same sign, and if M is increased as A and B approach.

It appears, therefore, that if we admit that the unresisted part of electromotive force goes on as long as it acts, generating a self-persistent state of the current, which we may call (from mechanical analogy) its electromagnetic momentum, and that this momentum depends on circumstances external to the conductor, then both induction of currents and electromagnetic attractions may be proved by mechanical reasoning.

What I have called electromagnetic momentum is the same quantity which is called by FARADAY[*] the electrotonic state of the circuit, every change of which involves the action of an electromotive force, just as change of momentum involves the action of mechanical force.

If, therefore, the phenomena described by FARADAY in the Ninth Series of his Experimental Researches were the only known facts about electric currents, the laws of AMPÈRE relating to the attraction of conductors carrying currents, as well as those of FARADAY about the mutual induction of currents, might be deduced by mechanical reasoning.

In order to bring these results within the range of experimental verification, I shall next investigate the case of a single current, of two currents, and of the six currents in the electric balance, so as to enable the experimenter to determine the values of L, M, N.

[*] Experimental Researches, Series I. 60, &c.

Case of a single Circuit.

(35) The equation of the current x in a circuit whose resistance is R, and whose coefficient of self-induction is L, acted on by an external electromotive force ξ, is

$$\xi - Rx = \frac{d}{dt} Lx. \quad \ldots \quad \ldots \quad \ldots \quad (13)$$

When ξ is constant, the solution is of the form

$$x = b + (a-b)e^{-\frac{R}{L}t},$$

where a is the value of the current at the commencement, and b is its final value.

The total quantity of electricity which passes in time t, where t is great, is

$$\int_0^t x\,dt = bt + (a-b)\frac{L}{R}. \quad \ldots \quad \ldots \quad \ldots \quad (14)$$

The value of the integral of x^2 with respect to the time is

$$\int_0^t x^2\,dt = b^2 t + (a-b)\frac{L}{R}\left(\frac{3b+a}{2}\right). \quad \ldots \quad \ldots \quad (15)$$

The actual current changes gradually from. the initial value a to the final value b, but the values of the integrals of x and x^2 are the same as if a steady current of intensity $\frac{1}{2}(a+b)$ were to flow for a time $2\frac{L}{R}$, and were then succeeded by the steady current b. The time $2\frac{L}{R}$ is generally so minute a fraction of a second, that the effects on the galvanometer and dynamometer may be calculated as if the impulse were instantaneous.

If the circuit consists of a battery and a coil, then, when the circuit is first completed, the effects are the same as if the current had only half its final strength during the time $2\frac{L}{R}$. This diminution of the current, due to induction, is sometimes called the counter-current.

(36) If an additional resistance. r is suddenly thrown into the circuit, as by breaking contact, so as. to force the current to pass through a thin wire of resistance r, then the original current is $a = \frac{\xi}{R}$, and the final current. is $b = \frac{\xi}{R+r}$.

The current of induction is then $\frac{1}{2}\xi\frac{2R+r}{R(R+r)}$, and continues for a time $2\frac{L}{R+r}$. This current is. greater than that which the battery can maintain in the two wires R and.r, and may be sufficient to ignite the thin wire r.

When contact is broken by separating the wires in air, this additional resistance is given by the interposed air, and since the electromotive force across the new resistance is very great, a spark will be forced across.

If the electromotive force is of the form $E \sin pt$, as in the case of a coil revolving in a magnetic field, then

$$x = \frac{E}{\varrho} \sin(pt - \alpha),$$

where $\varrho^2 = R^2 + L^2 p^2$, and $\tan \alpha = \frac{Lp}{R}$.

Case of two Circuits.

(37) Let R be the primary circuit and S the secondary circuit, then we have a case similar to that of the induction coil.

The equations of currents are those marked A and B, and we may here assume L, M, N as constant because there is no motion of the conductors. The equations then become

$$\left. \begin{array}{l} Rx + L\frac{dx}{dt} + M\frac{dy}{dt} = \xi, \\[2mm] Sy + M\frac{dx}{dt} + N\frac{dy}{dt} = 0. \end{array} \right\} \quad \ldots \ldots \quad (13^*)$$

To find the total quantity of electricity which passes, we have only to integrate these equations with respect to t; then if x_0, y_0 be the strengths of the currents at time 0, and x_1, y_1 at time t, and if X, Y be the quantities of electricity passed through each circuit during time t,

$$\left. \begin{array}{l} X = \frac{1}{R}\{\xi t + L(x_0 - x_1) + M(y_0 - y_1)\}, \\[2mm] Y = \frac{1}{S}\{M(x_0 - x_1) + N(y_0 - y_1)\}. \end{array} \right\} \quad \ldots \ldots \quad (14^*)$$

When the circuit R is completed, then the total currents up to time t, when t is great, are found by making

$$x_0 = 0, \quad x_1 = \frac{\xi}{R}, \quad y_0 = 0, \quad y_1 = 0;$$

then

$$X = x_1\left(t - \frac{L}{R}\right), \quad Y = -\frac{M}{S}x_1. \quad \ldots \ldots \quad (15^*)$$

The value of the total counter-current in R is therefore independent of the secondary circuit, and the induction current in the secondary circuit depends only on M, the coefficient of induction between the coils, S the resistance of the secondary coil, and x_1 the final strength of the current in R.

When the electromotive force ξ ceases to act, there is an extra current in the primary circuit, and a positive induced current in the secondary circuit, whose values are equal and opposite to those produced on making contact.

(38) All questions relating to the total quantity of transient currents, as measured by the impulse given to the magnet of the galvanometer, may be solved in this way without the necessity of a complete solution of the equations. The heating effect of

the current, and the impulse it gives to the suspended coil of WEBER's dynamometer, depend on the square of the current at every instant during the short time it lasts. Hence we must obtain the solution of the equations, and from the solution we may find the effects both on the galvanometer and dynamometer; and we may then make use of the method of WEBER for estimating the intensity and duration of a current uniform while it lasts which would produce the same effects.

(39) Let n_1, n_2 be the roots of the equation

$$(LN-M^2)n^2+(RN+LS)n+RS=0, \quad \ldots \ldots \ldots (16)$$

and let the primary coil be acted on by a constant electromotive force Rc, so that c is the constant current it could maintain; then the complete solution of the equations for making contact is

$$x=\frac{c}{S}\frac{n_1 n_2}{n_1-n_2}\left\{\left(\frac{S}{n_1}+N\right)e^{n_1 t}-\left(\frac{S}{n_2}+N\right)e^{n_2 t}+S\frac{n_1-n_2}{n_1 n_2}\right\}, \quad \ldots \ldots (17)$$

$$y=\frac{cM}{S}\frac{n_1 n_2}{n_1-n_2}\{e^{n_1 t}-e^{n_2 t}\}. \quad \ldots \ldots \ldots \ldots \ldots (18)$$

From these we obtain for calculating the impulse on the dynamometer,

$$\int x^2 dt=c^2\left\{t-\tfrac{3}{2}\frac{L}{R}-\tfrac{1}{2}\frac{M^2}{RN+LS}\right\}, \quad \ldots \ldots \ldots (19)$$

$$\int y^2 dt=c^2\tfrac{1}{2}\frac{M^2 R}{S(RN+LS)}. \quad \ldots \ldots \ldots (20)$$

The effects of the current in the secondary coil on the galvanometer and dynamometer are the same as those of a uniform current

$$-\tfrac{1}{2}c\frac{MR}{RN+LS}$$

for a time

$$2\left(\frac{L}{R}+\frac{N}{S}\right).$$

(40) The equation between work and energy may be easily verified. The work done by the electromotive force is

$$\xi\int x dt=c^2(Rt-L).$$

Work done in overcoming resistance and producing heat,

$$R\int x^2 dt+S\int y^2 dt=c^2(Rt-\tfrac{3}{2}L).$$

Energy remaining in the system,

$$=\tfrac{1}{2}c^2 L.$$

(41) If the circuit R is suddenly and completely interrupted while carrying a current c, then the equation of the current in the secondary coil would be

$$y=c\frac{M}{N}e^{-\frac{S}{N}t}.$$

This current begins with a value $c\frac{M}{N}$, and gradually disappears.

The total quantity of electricity is $c\dfrac{M}{S}$, and the value of $\int y^2 dt$ is $c^2\dfrac{M^2}{2SN}$.

The effects on the galvanometer and dynamometer are equal to those of a uniform current $\tfrac{1}{2}c\dfrac{M}{N}$ for a time $2\dfrac{N}{S}$.

The heating effect is therefore greater than that of the current on making contact.

(42) If an electromotive force of the form $\xi = E\cos pt$ acts on the circuit R, then if the circuit S is removed, the value of x will be

$$x = \frac{E}{A}\sin(pt - \alpha),$$

where

and

$$A^2 = R^2 + L^2 p^2,$$

$$\tan\alpha = \frac{Lp}{R}.$$

The effect of the presence of the circuit S in the neighbourhood is to alter the value of A and α, to that which they would be if R become

$$R + p^2\frac{MS}{S^2 + p^2 N^2},$$

and L became

$$L - p^2\frac{MN}{S^2 + p^2 N^2}.$$

Hence the effect of the presence of the circuit S is to increase the apparent resistance and diminish the apparent self-induction of the circuit R.

On the Determination of Coefficients of Induction by the Electric Balance.

(43) The electric balance consists of six conductors joining four points, A C D E, two and two. One pair, A C, of these points is connected through the battery B. The opposite pair, D E, is connected through the galvanometer G. Then if the resistances of the four remaining conductors are represented by P, Q, R, S, and the currents in them by x, $x-z$, y, and $y+z$, the current through G will be z. Let the potentials at the four points be A, C, D, E. Then the conditions of steady currents may be found from the equations

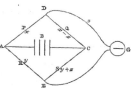

$$
\left.
\begin{aligned}
Px &= A - D & Q(x-z) &= D - C, \\
Ry &= A - E & S(y+z) &= E - C, \\
Gz &= D - E & B(x+y) &= -A + C + F.
\end{aligned}
\right\} \qquad \cdots \cdots \cdots \quad (21)
$$

Solving these equations for z, we find

$$z\left\{\frac{1}{P}+\frac{1}{Q}+\frac{1}{R}+\frac{1}{S}+B\left(\frac{1}{P}+\frac{1}{R}\right)\left(\frac{1}{Q}+\frac{1}{S}\right)+G\left(\frac{1}{P}+\frac{1}{Q}\right)\left(\frac{1}{R}+\frac{1}{S}\right)+\frac{BG}{PQRS}(P+Q+R+S)\right\}=F\left(\frac{1}{PS}-\frac{1}{QR}\right). \quad (22)$$

In this expression F is the electromotive force of the battery, z the current through the galvanometer when it has become steady. P, Q, R, S the resistances in the four arms. B that of the battery and electrodes, and G that of the galvanometer.

(44) If PS=QR, then $z=0$, and there will be no steady current, but a transient current through the galvanometer may be produced on making or breaking circuit on account of induction, and the indications of the galvanometer may be used to determine the coefficients of induction, provided we understand the actions which take place.

We shall suppose PS=QR, so that the current z vanishes when sufficient time is allowed, and

$$x(P+Q)=y(R+S)= \frac{F(P+Q)(R+S)}{(P+Q)(R+S)+B(P+Q)(R+S)}.$$

Let the induction coefficients between P, Q, R S, be given by the following Table, the coefficient of induction of P on itself being p, between P and Q, h, and so on.

Let g be the coefficient of induction of the galvanometer on itself, and let it be out of the reach of the inductive influence of P, Q, R, S (as it must be in order to avoid

	P	Q	R	S
P	p	h	k	l
Q	h	q	m	n
R	k	m	r	o
S	l	n	o	s

direct action of P, Q, R, S on the needle). Let X, Y, Z be the integrals of x, y, z with respect to t. At making contact x, y, z are zero. After a time z disappears, and x and y reach constant values. The equations for each conductor will therefore be

$$
\begin{aligned}
\text{PX} & +(p+h\ )x+(k+l\ )y=\int A dt-\int D dt, \\
\text{Q(X}-\text{Z)} &+(h+q\ )x+(m+n)y=\int D dt-\int C dt, \\
\text{RY} & +(k+m)x+(r\ +o)y=\int A dt-\int E dt, \\
\text{S(Y}+\text{Z)} &+(l+n\ )x+(o\ +s)y=\int E dt-\int C dt, \\
\text{GZ} &=\int D t d-\int E dt.
\end{aligned}
\qquad \cdots \quad (24)
$$

Solving these equations for Z, we find

$$
\begin{aligned}
\text{Z}&\left\{\frac{1}{P}+\frac{1}{Q}+\frac{1}{R}+\frac{1}{S}+B\left(\frac{1}{P}+\frac{1}{R}\right)\left(\frac{1}{Q}+\frac{1}{S}\right)+G\left(\frac{1}{P}+\frac{1}{Q}\right)\left(\frac{1}{R}+\frac{1}{S}\right)+\frac{BG}{PQRS}(P+Q+R+S)\right\} \\
&=-F\frac{1}{PS}\left\{\frac{p}{P}-\frac{q}{Q}-\frac{r}{R}+\frac{s}{S}+h\left(\frac{1}{P}-\frac{1}{Q}\right)+k\left(\frac{1}{R}-\frac{1}{P}\right)+l\left(\frac{1}{R}+\frac{1}{Q}\right)-m\left(\frac{1}{P}+\frac{1}{S}\right)\right. \\
&\left.+n\left(\frac{1}{Q}-\frac{1}{S}\right)+o\left(\frac{1}{S}-\frac{1}{R}\right)\right\}.
\end{aligned}
\qquad (25)
$$

(45) Now let the deflection of the galvanometer by the instantaneous current whose intensity is Z be α.

Let the permanent deflection produced by making the ratio of PS to QR, ϱ instead of unity, be θ.

Also let the time of vibration of the galvanometer needle from rest to rest be T.

Then calling the quantity

$$\frac{p}{P}-\frac{q}{Q}-\frac{r}{R}+\frac{s}{S}+h\left(\frac{1}{P}-\frac{1}{Q}\right)+k\left(\frac{1}{R}-\frac{1}{P}\right)+l\left(\frac{1}{R}+\frac{1}{Q}\right)-m\left(\frac{1}{P}+\frac{1}{S}\right)+n\left(\frac{1}{Q}-\frac{1}{S}\right)+o\left(\frac{1}{S}-\frac{1}{R}\right)=\tau, \quad (26)$$

we find

$$\frac{Z}{z}=\frac{2\sin\frac12\alpha}{\tan\theta}\,\frac{T}{\pi}=\frac{\tau}{1-\varrho}. \quad\ldots\ldots\ldots (27)$$

In determining τ by experiment, it is best to make the alteration of resistance in one of the arms by means of the arrangement described by Mr. JENKIN in the Report of the British Association for 1863, by which any value of ϱ from 1 to 1·01 can be accurately measured.

We observe (α) the greatest deflection due to the impulse of induction when the galvanometer is in circuit, when the connexions are made, and when the resistances are so adjusted as to give no permanent current.

We then observe (β) the greatest deflection produced by the permanent current when the resistance of one of the arms is increased in the ratio of 1 to ϱ, the galvanometer not being in circuit till a little while after the connexion is made with the battery.

In order to eliminate the effects of resistance of the air, it is best to vary ϱ till $\beta=2\alpha$ nearly; then

$$\tau=T\frac{1}{\pi}(1-\varrho)\frac{2\sin\frac12\alpha}{\tan\frac12\beta}. \quad\ldots\ldots\ldots (28)$$

If all the arms of the balance except P consist of resistance coils of very fine wire of no great length and doubled before being coiled, the induction coefficients belonging to these coils will be insensible, and τ will be reduced to $\frac{p}{P}$. The electric balance therefore affords the means of measuring the self-induction of any circuit whose resistance is known.

(46) It may also be used to determine the coefficient of induction between two circuits, as for instance, that between P and S which we have called $\dot m$; but it would be more convenient to measure this by directly measuring the current, as in (37), without using the balance. We may also ascertain the equality of $\frac{p}{P}$ and $\frac{q}{Q}$ by there being no current of induction, and thus, when we know the value of p, we may determine that of q by a more perfect method than the comparison of deflections.

Exploration of the Electromagnetic Field.

(47) Let us now suppose the primary circuit A to be of invariable form, and let us explore the electromagnetic field by means of the secondary circuit B, which we shall suppose to be variable in form and position.

We may begin by supposing B to consist of a short straight conductor with its extremities sliding on two parallel conducting rails, which are put in connexion at some distance from the sliding-piece.

Then, if sliding the moveable conductor in a given direction increases the value of M, a negative electromotive force will act in the circuit B, tending to produce a negative current in B during the motion of the sliding-piece.

If a current be kept up in the circuit B, then the sliding-piece will itself tend to move in that direction, which causes M to increase. At every point of the field there will always be a certain direction such that a conductor moved in that direction does not experience any electromotive force in whatever direction its extremities are turned. A conductor carrying a current will experience no mechanical force urging it in that direction or the opposite.

This direction is called the direction of the line of magnetic force through that point.

Motion of a conductor across such a line produces electromotive force in a direction perpendicular to the line and to the direction of motion, and a conductor carrying a current is urged in a direction perpendicular to the line and to the direction of the current.

(48) We may next suppose B to consist of a very small plane circuit capable of being placed in any position and of having its plane turned in any direction. The value of M will be greatest when the plane of the circuit is perpendicular to the line of magnetic force. Hence if a current is maintained in B it will tend to set itself in this position, and will of itself indicate, like a magnet, the direction of the magnetic force.

On Lines of Magnetic Force.

(49) Let any surface be drawn, cutting the lines of magnetic force, and on this surface let any system of lines be drawn at small intervals, so as to lie side by side without cutting each other.   Next, let any line be drawn on the surface cutting all these lines, and let a second line be drawn near it, its distance from the first being such that the value of M for each of the small spaces enclosed between these two lines and the lines of the first system is equal to unity.

In this way let more lines be drawn so as to form a second system, so that the value of M for every reticulation formed by the intersection of the two systems of lines is unity.

Finally, from every point of intersection of these reticulations let a line be drawn through the field, always coinciding in direction with the direction of magnetic force.

(50) In this way the whole field will be filled with lines of magnetic force at regular intervals, and the properties of the electromagnetic field will be completely expressed by them.

For, 1st, If any closed curve be drawn in the field, the value of M for that curve will be expressed by the *number* of lines of force which *pass through* that closed curve.

2ndly. If this curve be a conducting circuit and be moved through the field, an electromotive force will act in it, represented by the rate of decrease of the number of lines passing through the curve.

3rdly. If a current be maintained in the circuit, the conductor will be acted on by forces tending to move it so as to increase the number of lines passing through it, and the amount of work done by these forces is equal to the current in the circuit multiplied by the number of additional lines.

4thly. If a small plane circuit be placed in the field, and be free to turn, it will place its plane perpendicular to the lines of force. A small magnet will place itself with its axis in the direction of the lines of force.

5thly. If a long uniformly magnetized bar is placed in the field, each pole will be acted on by a force in the direction of the lines of force. The number of lines of force passing through unit of area is equal to the force acting on a unit pole multiplied by a coefficient depending on the magnetic nature of the medium, and called the coefficient of magnetic induction.

In fluids and isotropic solids the value of this coefficient μ is the same in whatever direction the lines of force pass through the substance, but in crystallized, strained, and organized solids the value of μ may depend on the direction of the lines of force with respect to the axes of crystallization, strain, or growth.

In all bodies μ is affected by temperature, and in iron it appears to diminish as the intensity of the magnetization increases.

On Magnetic Equipotential Surfaces.

(51) If we explore the field with a uniformly magnetized bar, so long that one of its poles is in a very weak part of the magnetic field, then the magnetic forces will perform work on the other pole as it moves about the field.

If we start from a given point, and move this pole from it to any other point, the work performed will be independent of the path of the pole between the two points; provided that no electric current passes between the different paths pursued by the pole.

Hence, when there are no electric currents but only magnets in the field, we may draw a series of surfaces such that the work done in passing from one to another shall be constant whatever be the path pursued between them. Such surfaces are called Equipotential Surfaces, and in ordinary cases are perpendicular to the Lines of magnetic force.

If these surfaces are so drawn that, when a unit pole passes from any one to the next in order, unity of work is done, then the work done in any motion of a magnetic pole will be measured by the strength of the pole multiplied by the number of surfaces which it has passed through in the positive direction.

(52) If there are circuits carrying electric currents in the field, then there will still be equipotential surfaces in the parts of the field external to the conductors carrying the currents, but the work done on a unit pole in passing from one to another will depend on the number of times which the path of the pole circulates round any of these currents. Hence the potential in each surface will have a series of values in arithmetical progression, differing by the work done in passing completely round one of the currents in the field.

The equipotential surfaces will not be continuous closed surfaces, but some of them will be limited sheets, terminating in the electric circuit as their common edge or boundary. The number of these will be equal to the amount of work done on a unit pole in going round the current, and this by the ordinary measurement $=4\pi\gamma$, where γ is the value of the current.

These surfaces, therefore, are connected with the electric current as soap-bubbles are connected with a ring in M. PLATEAU's experiments. Every current γ has $4\pi\gamma$ surfaces attached to it. These surfaces have the current for their common edge, and meet it at equal angles. The form of the surfaces in other parts depends on the presence of other currents and magnets, as well as on the shape of the circuit to which they belong.

PART III.—GENERAL EQUATIONS OF THE ELECTROMAGNETIC FIELD.

(53.) Let us assume three rectangular directions in space as the axes of x, y, and z, and let all quantities having direction be expressed by their components in these three directions.

Electrical Currents (p, q, r).

(54) An electrical current consists in the transmission of electricity from one part of a body to another. Let the quantity of electricity transmitted in unit of time across unit of area perpendicular to the axis of x be called p, then p is the component of the current at that place in the direction of x.

We shall use the letters p, q, r to denote the components of the current per unit of area in the directions of x, y, z.

Electrical Displacements (f, g, h).

(55) Electrical displacement consists in the opposite electrification of the sides of a molecule or particle of a body which may or may not be accompanied with transmission through the body. Let the quantity of electricity which would appear on the faces $dy.dz$ of an element dx, dy, dz cut from the body be $f.dy.dz$, then f is the component of electric displacement parallel to x. We shall use f, g, h to denote the electric displacements parallel to x, y, z respectively.

The variations of the electrical displacement must be added to the currents p, q, r to get the total motion of electricity, which we may call p', q', r', so that

$$\left.\begin{aligned} p' &= p + \frac{df}{dt}, \\ q' &= q + \frac{dg}{dt}, \\ r' &= r + \frac{dh}{dt}, \end{aligned}\right\} \quad \cdots \cdots \cdots \text{(A)}$$

Electromotive Force (P, Q, R).

(56) Let P, Q, R represent the components of the electromotive force at any point. Then P represents the difference of potential per unit of length in a conductor

placed in the direction of x at the given point. We may suppose an indefinitely short wire placed parallel to x at a given point and touched, during the action of the force P, by two small conductors, which are then insulated and removed from the influence of the electromotive force. The value of P might then be ascertained by measuring the charge of the conductors.

Thus if l be the length of the wire, the difference of potential at its ends will be Pl, and if C be the capacity of each of the small conductors the charge on each will be $\frac{1}{2}$CPl. Since the capacities of moderately large conductors, measured on the electromagnetic system, are exceedingly small, ordinary electromotive forces arising from electromagnetic actions could hardly be measured in this way. In practice such measurements are always made with long conductors, forming closed or nearly closed circuits.

Electromagnetic Momentum (F, G, H).

(57) Let F, G, H represent the components of electromagnetic momentum at any point of the field, due to any system of magnets or currents.

Then F is the total impulse of the electromotive force in the direction of x that would be generated by the removal of these magnets or currents from the field, that is, if P be the electromotive force at any instant during the removal of the system

$$F = \int P dt.$$

Hence the part of the electromotive force which depends on the motion of magnets or currents in the field, or their alteration of intensity, is

$$P = -\frac{dF}{dt}, \quad Q = -\frac{dG}{dt}, \quad R = -\frac{dH}{dt}. \quad \cdots \cdots \quad (29)$$

Electromagnetic Momentum of a Circuit.

(58) Let s be the length of the circuit, then if we integrate

$$\int \left(F \frac{dx}{ds} + G \frac{dy}{ds} + H \frac{dz}{ds} \right) ds \quad \cdots \cdots \cdots \cdots \quad (30)$$

round the circuit, we shall get the total electromagnetic momentum of the circuit, or the number of lines of magnetic force which pass through it, the variations of which measure the total electromotive force in the circuit. This electromagnetic momentum is the same thing to which Professor FARADAY has applied the name of the Electrotonic State.

If the circuit be the boundary of the elementary area $dy\, dz$, then its electromagnetic momentum is

$$\left(\frac{dH}{dy} - \frac{dG}{dz} \right) dy\, dz,$$

and this is the number of lines of magnetic force which pass through the area $dy\, dz$.

Magnetic Force (α, β, γ).

(59) Let α, β, γ represent the force acting on a unit magnetic pole placed at the given point resolved in the directions of x, y, and z.

Coefficient of Magnetic Induction (μ).

(60) Let μ be the ratio of the magnetic induction in a given medium to that in air under an equal magnetizing force, then the number of lines of force in unit of area perpendicular to x will be $\mu\alpha$ (μ is a quantity depending on the nature of the medium, its temperature, the amount of magnetization already produced, and in crystalline bodies varying with the direction).

(61) Expressing the electric momentum of small circuits perpendicular to the three axes in this notation, we obtain the following

Equations of Magnetic Force.

$$
\left.
\begin{aligned}
\mu\alpha &= \frac{d\mathrm{H}}{dy} - \frac{d\mathrm{G}}{dz}, \\
\mu\beta &= \frac{d\mathrm{F}}{dz} - \frac{d\mathrm{H}}{dx}, \\
\mu\gamma &= \frac{d\mathrm{G}}{dx} - \frac{d\mathrm{F}}{dy}.
\end{aligned}
\right\} \quad \dots \dots \dots \text{(B)}
$$

Equations of Currents.

(62) It is known from experiment that the motion of a magnetic pole in the electromagnetic field in a closed circuit cannot generate work unless the circuit which the pole describes passes round an electric current. Hence, except in the space occupied by the electric currents,

$$
\alpha dx + \beta dy + \gamma dz = d\varphi \quad \dots \dots \dots \text{(31)}
$$

a complete differential of φ, the magnetic potential.

The quantity φ may be susceptible of an indefinite number of distinct values, according to the number of times that the exploring point passes round electric currents in its course, the difference between successive values of φ corresponding to a passage completely round a current of strength c being $4\pi c$.

Hence if there is no electric current,

$$
dy - \frac{d\beta}{dz} = 0 ;
$$

but if there is a current p',

$$
\frac{d\gamma}{dy} - \frac{d\beta}{dz} = 4\pi p'.
$$

Similarly,

$$
\left.
\begin{aligned}
\frac{d\alpha}{dz} - \frac{d\gamma}{dx} &= 4\pi q', \\
\frac{d\beta}{dx} - \frac{d\alpha}{dy} &= 4\pi r'.
\end{aligned}
\right\} \quad \dots \dots \dots \text{(C)}
$$

We may call these the Equations of Currents.

Electromotive Force in a Circuit.

(63) Let ξ be the electromotive force acting round the circuit A, then

$$\xi = \int\left(P\frac{dx}{ds}+Q\frac{dy}{ds}+R\frac{dz}{ds}\right)ds, \quad \ldots \ldots \ldots (32)$$

where ds is the element of length, and the integration is performed round the circuit.

Let the forces in the field be those due to the circuits A and B, then the electro-magnetic momentum of A is

$$\int\left(F\frac{dx}{ds}+G\frac{dy}{ds}+H\frac{dz}{ds}\right)ds = Lu+Mv, \quad \ldots \ldots \ldots (33)$$

where u and v are the currents in A and B, and

$$\xi = -\frac{d}{dt}(Lu+Mv). \quad \ldots \ldots \ldots \ldots (34)$$

Hence, if there is no motion of the circuit A,

$$\left.\begin{array}{l} P = -\dfrac{dF}{dt}-\dfrac{d\Psi}{dx}, \\[2mm] Q = -\dfrac{dG}{dt}-\dfrac{d\Psi}{dy}, \\[2mm] R = -\dfrac{dH}{dt}-\dfrac{d\Psi}{dz}, \end{array}\right\} \quad \ldots \ldots \ldots (35)$$

where Ψ is a function of x, y, z, and t, which is indeterminate as far as regards the solution of the above equations, because the terms depending on it will disappear on integrating round the circuit. The quantity Ψ can always, however, be determined in any particular case when we know the actual conditions of the question. The physical interpretation of Ψ is, that it represents the *electric potential* at each point of space.

Electromotive Force on a Moving Conductor.

(64) Let a short straight conductor of length a, parallel to the axis of x, move with a velocity whose components are $\frac{dx}{dt}$, $\frac{dy}{dt}$, $\frac{dz}{dt}$, and let its extremities slide along two parallel conductors with a velocity $\frac{ds}{dt}$. Let us find the alteration of the electro-magnetic momentum of the circuit of which this arrangement forms a part.

In unit of time the moving conductor has travelled distances $\frac{dx}{dt}$, $\frac{dy}{dt}$, $\frac{dz}{dt}$ along the directions of the three axes, and at the same time the lengths of the parallel conductors included in the circuit have each been increased by $\frac{ds}{dt}$.

Hence the quantity

$$\int\left(F\frac{dx}{ds}+G\frac{dy}{ds}+H\frac{dz}{ds}\right)ds$$

will be increased by the following increments,

$$a\left(\frac{d\mathrm{F}}{dx}\frac{dx}{dt}+\frac{d\mathrm{F}}{dy}\frac{dy}{dt}+\frac{d\mathrm{F}}{dz}\frac{dz}{dt}\right), \text{ due to motion of conductor,}$$

$$-a\frac{ds}{dt}\left(\frac{d\mathrm{F}}{dx}\frac{dx}{ds}+\frac{d\mathrm{G}}{dx}\frac{dy}{ds}+\frac{d\mathrm{H}}{dx}\frac{dz}{ds}\right), \text{ due to lengthening of circuit.}$$

The total increment will therefore be

$$a\left(\frac{d\mathrm{F}}{dy}-\frac{d\mathrm{G}}{dx}\right)\frac{dy}{dt}-a\left(\frac{d\mathrm{H}}{dx}-\frac{d\mathrm{F}}{dz}\right)\frac{dz}{dt};$$

or, by the equations of Magnetic Force (8),

$$-a\left(\mu\gamma\frac{dy}{dt}-\mu\beta\frac{dz}{dt}\right).$$

If P is the electromotive force in the moving conductor parallel to x referred to unit of length, then the actual electromotive force is Pa; and since this is measured by the decrement of the electromagnetic momentum of the circuit, the electromotive force due to motion will be

$$\mathrm{P}=\mu\gamma\frac{dy}{dt}-\mu\beta\frac{dz}{dt}. \quad \cdot \quad \cdot \quad \cdot \quad \cdot \quad \cdot \quad \cdot \quad (36)$$

(65) The complete equations of electromotive force on a moving conductor may now be written as follows:—

Equations of Electromotive Force.

$$\left.\begin{array}{l}
\mathrm{P}=\mu\left(\gamma\frac{dy}{dt}-\beta\frac{dz}{dt}\right)-\frac{d\mathrm{F}}{dt}-\frac{d\Psi}{dx}, \\[2mm]
\mathrm{Q}=\mu\left(\alpha\frac{dz}{dt}-\gamma\frac{dx}{dt}\right)-\frac{d\mathrm{G}}{dt}-\frac{d\Psi}{dy}, \\[2mm]
\mathrm{R}=\mu\left(\beta\frac{dx}{dt}-\alpha\frac{dy}{dt}\right)-\frac{d\mathrm{H}}{dt}-\frac{d\Psi}{dz}.
\end{array}\right\} \quad \cdot \quad \cdot \quad \cdot \quad \cdot \quad (\mathrm{D})$$

The first term on the right-hand side of each equation represents the electromotive force arising from the motion of the conductor itself. This electromotive force is perpendicular to the direction of motion and to the lines of magnetic force; and if a parallelogram be drawn whose sides represent in direction and magnitude the velocity of the conductor and the magnetic induction at that point of the field, then the area of the parallelogram will represent the electromotive force due to the motion of the conductor, and the direction of the force is perpendicular to the plane of the parallelogram.

The second term in each equation indicates the effect of changes in the position or strength of magnets or currents in the field.

The third term shows the effect of the electric potential Ψ. It has no effect in causing a circulating current in a closed circuit. It indicates the existence of a force urging the electricity to or from certain definite points in the field.

Electric Elasticity.

(66) When an electromotive force acts on a dielectric, it puts every part of the dielectric into a polarized condition, in which its opposite sides are oppositely electrified. The amount of this electrification depends on the electromotive force and on the nature of the substance, and, in solids having a structure defined by axes, on the direction of the electromotive force with respect to these axes. In isotropic substances, if k is the ratio of the electromotive force to the electric displacement, we may write the

Equations of Electric Elasticity,

$$\left. \begin{array}{l} P = kf, \\ Q = kg, \\ R = kh. \end{array} \right\} \quad \cdots \cdots \cdots \cdots \quad (E)$$

Electric Resistance.

(67) When an electromotive force acts on a conductor it produces a current of electricity through it. This effect is additional to the electric displacement already considered. In solids of complex structure, the relation between the electromotive force and the current depends on their direction through the solid. In isotropic substances, which alone we shall here consider, if ϱ is the specific resistance referred to unit of volume, we may write the

Equations of Electric Resistance,

$$\left. \begin{array}{l} P = -\varrho p, \\ Q = -\varrho q, \\ R = -\varrho r. \end{array} \right\} \quad \cdots \cdots \cdots \cdots \quad (F)$$

Electric Quantity.

(68) Let e represent the quantity of free positive electricity contained in unit of volume at any part of the field, then, since this arises from the electrification of the different parts of the field not neutralizing each other, we may write the

Equation of Free Electricity,

$$e + \frac{df}{dx} + \frac{dg}{dy} + \frac{dh}{dz} = 0. \quad \cdots \cdots \cdots \quad (G)$$

(69) If the medium conducts electricity, then we shall have another condition, which may be called, as in hydrodynamics, the

Equation of Continuity,

$$\frac{de}{dt} + \frac{dp}{dx} + \frac{dq}{dy} + \frac{dr}{dz} = 0. \quad \cdots \cdots \cdots \quad (H)$$

(70) In these equations of the electromagnetic field we have assumed twenty variable

quantities, namely,

For Electromagnetic Momentum . . . . F   G   H
 ,, Magnetic Intensity . . . . α β γ
 ,, Electromotive Force . . . . P   Q   R
 ,, Current due to true conduction. . . . . p q r
 ,, Electric Displacement. . . . . f g h
 ,, Total Current (including variation of displacement) . . p' q' r'
 ,, Quantity of free Electricity . . . . e
 ,, Electric Potential . . . . Ψ

Between these twenty quantities we have found twenty equations, viz.

Three equations of Magnetic Force . . . . (B)
     ,,   Electric Currents. . . . . (C)
     ,,   Electromotive Force . . . . (D)
     ,,   Electric Elasticity . . . . (E)
     ,,   Electric Resistance . . . . (F)
     ,,   Total Currents . . . . (A)
One equation of Free Electricity . . . . (G)
     ,,   Continuity . . . . (H)

These equations are therefore sufficient to determine all the quantities which occur in them, provided we know the conditions of the problem. In many questions, however, only a few of the equations are required.

Intrinsic Energy of the Electromagnetic Field.

(71) We have seen (33) that the intrinsic energy of any system of currents is found by multiplying half the current in each circuit into its electromagnetic momentum. This is equivalent to finding the integral

$$E = \tfrac{1}{2}\Sigma(Fp' + Gq' + Hr')dV \quad . . . . \quad (37)$$

over all the space occupied by currents, where p, q, r are the components of currents, and F, G, H the components of electromagnetic momentum.

Substituting the values of p', q', r' from the equations of Currents (C), this becomes

$$\frac{1}{8\pi}\Sigma\left\{F\left(\frac{d\gamma}{dy}-\frac{d\beta}{dz}\right)+G\left(\frac{d\alpha}{dz}-\frac{d\gamma}{dx}\right)+H\left(\frac{d\beta}{dx}-\frac{d\alpha}{dy}\right)\right\}dV.$$

Integrating by parts, and remembering that α, β, γ vanish at an infinite distance, the expression becomes

$$\frac{1}{8\pi}\Sigma\left\{\alpha\left(\frac{dH}{dy}-\frac{dG}{dz}\right)+\beta\left(\frac{dF}{dz}-\frac{dH}{dx}\right)+\gamma\left(\frac{dG}{dx}-\frac{dF}{dy}\right)\right\}dV,$$

where the integration is to be extended over all space. Referring to the equations of Magnetic Force (B), p. 482, this becomes

$$E = \frac{1}{8\pi}\Sigma\{\alpha.\mu\alpha + \beta.\mu\beta + \gamma.\mu\gamma\}dV, \quad . . . . \quad (38)$$

where α, β, γ are the components of magnetic intensity or the force on a unit magnetic pole, and $\mu\alpha$, $\mu\beta$, $\mu\gamma$ are the components of the quantity of magnetic induction, or the number of lines of force in unit of area.

In isotropic media the value of μ is the same in all directions, and we may express the result more simply by saying that the intrinsic energy of any part of the magnetic field arising from its magnetization is

$$\frac{\mu}{8\pi}I^2$$

per unit of volume, where I is the magnetic intensity.

(72) Energy may be stored up in the field in a different way, namely, by the action of electromotive force in producing electric displacement. The work done by a variable electromotive force, P, in producing a variable displacement, f, is got by integrating

$$\int P df$$

from P$=0$ to the given value of P.

Since P$=kf$, equation (E), this quantity becomes

$$\int kf df = \tfrac{1}{2}kf^2 = \tfrac{1}{2}Pf.$$

Hence the intrinsic energy of any part of the field, as existing in the form of electric displacement, is

$$\tfrac{1}{2}\Sigma(Pf+Qg+Rh)dV.$$

The total energy existing in the field is therefore

$$E=\Sigma\left\{\frac{1}{8\pi}(\alpha\mu\alpha+\beta\mu\beta+\gamma\mu\gamma)+\tfrac{1}{2}(Pf+Qg+Rh)\right\}dV. \quad . \quad . \quad . \quad . \quad \text{(I)}$$

The first term of this expression depends on the magnetization of the field, and is explained on our theory by actual motion of some kind. The second term depends on the electric polarization of the field, and is explained on our theory by strain of some kind in an elastic medium.

(73) I have on a former occasion* attempted to describe a particular kind of motion and a particular kind of strain, so arranged as to account for the phenomena. In the present paper I avoid any hypothesis of this kind; and in using such words as electric momentum and electric elasticity in reference to the known phenomena of the induction of currents and the polarization of dielectrics, I wish merely to direct the mind of the reader to mechanical phenomena which will assist him in understanding the electrical ones. All such phrases in the present paper are to be considered as illustrative, not as explanatory.

(74) In speaking of the Energy of the field, however, I wish to be understood literally. All energy is the same as mechanical energy, whether it exists in the form of motion or in that of elasticity, or in any other form. The energy in electromagnetic phenomena is mechanical energy. The only question is, Where does it reside? On the old theories

* " On Physical Lines of Force," Philosophical Magazine, 1861–62.

it resides in the electrified bodies, conducting circuits, and magnets, in the form of an unknown quality called potential energy, or the power of producing certain effects at a distance. On our theory it resides in the electromagnetic field, in the space surrounding the electrified and magnetic bodies, as well as in those bodies themselves, and is in two different forms, which may be described without hypothesis as magnetic polarization and electric polarization; or, according to a very probable hypothesis, as the motion and the strain of one and the same medium.

(75) The conclusions arrived at in the present paper are independent of this hypothesis, being deduced from experimental facts of three kinds:—

1. The induction of electric currents by the increase or diminution of neighbouring currents according to the changes in the lines of force passing through the circuit.

2. The distribution of magnetic intensity according to the variations of a magnetic potential.

3. The induction (or influence) of statical electricity through dielectrics.

We may now proceed to demonstrate from these principles the existence and laws of the mechanical forces which act upon electric currents, magnets, and electrified bodies placed in the electromagnetic field.

PART IV.—MECHANICAL ACTIONS IN THE FIELD.

Mechanical Force on a Moveable Conductor.

(76) We have shown (§§ 34 & 35) that the work done by the electromagnetic forces in aiding the motion of a conductor is equal to the product of the current in the conductor multiplied by the increment of the electromagnetic momentum due to the motion.

Let a short straight conductor of length a move parallel to itself in the direction of x, with its extremities on two parallel conductors. Then the increment of the electromagnetic momentum due to the motion of a will be

$$a\left(\frac{dF}{dx}\frac{dx}{ds}+\frac{dG}{dx}\frac{dy}{ds}+\frac{dH}{dx}\frac{dz}{ds}\right)\delta x.$$

That due to the lengthening of the circuit by increasing the length of the parallel conductors will be

$$-a\left(\frac{dF}{dx}\frac{dx}{ds}+\frac{dF}{dy}\frac{dy}{ds}+\frac{dF}{dz}\frac{dz}{ds}\right)\delta x.$$

The total increment is

$$a\delta x\left\{\frac{dy}{ds}\left(\frac{dG}{dx}-\frac{dF}{dy}\right)-\frac{dz}{ds}\left(\frac{dF}{dz}-\frac{dH}{dx}\right)\right\},$$

which is by the equations of Magnetic Force (B), p. 482,

$$a\delta x\left(\frac{dy}{ds}\mu\gamma-\frac{dz}{ds}\mu\beta\right).$$

Let X be the force acting along the direction of x per unit of length of the conductor, then the work done is $X a\delta x$.

Let C be the current in the conductor, and let p', q', r' be its components, then

$$X a \delta = C a \delta x x \left(\frac{dy}{ds} \mu \gamma - \frac{dz}{ds} \mu \beta \right),$$

or

$$X = \mu \gamma q' - \mu \beta r'.$$

Similarly,

$$Y = \mu \alpha r' - \mu \gamma p', \qquad \qquad \qquad \qquad \text{(J)}$$

$$Z = \mu \beta p' - \mu \alpha q'.$$

These are the equations which determine the mechanical force acting on a conductor carrying a current. The force is perpendicular to the current and to the lines of force, and is measured by the area of the parallelogram formed by lines parallel to the current and lines of force, and proportional to their intensities.

Mechanical Force on a Magnet.

(77) In any part of the field not traversed by electric currents the distribution of magnetic intensity may be represented by the differential coefficients of a function which may be called the magnetic potential. When there are no currents in the field, this quantity has a single value for each point. When there are currents, the potential has a series of values at each point, but its differential coefficients have only one value, namely,

$$\frac{d\varphi}{dx} = \alpha, \quad \frac{d\varphi}{dy} = \beta, \quad \frac{d\varphi}{dz} = \gamma.$$

Substituting these values of α, β, γ in the expression (equation 38) for the intrinsic energy of the field, and integrating by parts, it becomes

$$- \Sigma \left\{ \varphi \, \frac{1}{8\pi} \left(\frac{d\mu\alpha}{dx} + \frac{d\mu\beta}{dy} + \frac{d\mu\gamma}{dz} \right) \right\} d\mathrm{V}.$$

The expression

$$\Sigma \left(\frac{d\mu\alpha}{dx} + \frac{d\mu\beta}{dy} + \frac{d\mu\gamma}{dz} \right) d\mathrm{V} = \Sigma m d\mathrm{V} \qquad \cdots \cdots \text{(39)}$$

indicates the number of lines of magnetic force which have their origin within the space V. Now a magnetic pole is known to us only as the origin or termination of lines of magnetic force, and a unit pole is one which has 4π lines belonging to it, since it produces unit of magnetic intensity at unit of distance over a sphere whose surface is 4π.

Hence if m is the amount of free positive magnetism in unit of volume, the above expression may be written $4\pi m$, and the expression for the energy of the field becomes

$$\mathrm{E} = - \Sigma (\tfrac{1}{2}\varphi m) d\mathrm{V}. \qquad \cdots \cdots \cdots \text{(40)}$$

If there are two magnetic poles m_1 and m_2 producing potentials φ_1 and φ_2 in the field, then if m_2 is moved a distance dx, and is urged in that direction by a force X, then the work done is Xdx, and the decrease of energy in the field is

$$d\left(\tfrac{1}{2}(\varphi_1 + \varphi_2)(m_1 + m_2) \right),$$

and these must be equal by the principle of Conservation of Energy.

Since the distribution φ_1 is determined by m_1, and φ_2 by m_2, the quantities $\varphi_1 m_1$ and $\varphi_2 m_2$ will remain constant.

It can be shown also, as GREEN has proved (Essay, p. 10), that

$$m_1\varphi_2 = m_2\varphi_1,$$

so that we get

$$\mathrm{X}dx = d(m_2\varphi_1),$$

or

$$\mathrm{X} = m_2\frac{d\varphi_1}{dx} = m_2\alpha_1,$$

where α_1 represents the magnetic intensity due to m_1. . . . . (K)

Similarly,

$$\mathrm{Y} = m_2\beta_1,$$
$$\mathrm{Z} = m_2\gamma_1.$$

So that a magnetic pole is urged in the direction of the lines of magnetic force with a force equal to the product of the strength of the pole and the magnetic intensity.

(78) If a single magnetic pole, that is one pole of a very long magnet, be placed in the field, the only solution of φ is

$$\varphi_1 = -\frac{m_1}{\mu}\frac{1}{r}, \quad . \quad . \quad . \quad . \quad . \quad . \quad . \quad . \quad . \quad . \quad . \quad (41)$$

where m_1 is the strength of the pole and r the distance from it.

The repulsion between two poles of strength m_1 and m_2 is

$$m_2\frac{d\varphi_1}{dr} = \frac{m_1 m_2}{\mu r^2}. \quad . \quad . \quad . \quad . \quad . \quad . \quad . \quad . \quad . \quad (42)$$

In air or any medium in which $\mu = 1$ this is simply $\frac{m_1 m_2}{r^2}$, but in other media the force acting between two given magnetic poles is inversely proportional to the coefficient of magnetic induction for the medium. This may be explained by the magnetization of the medium induced by the action of the poles.

Mechanical Force on an Electrified Body.

(79) If there is no motion or change of strength of currents or magnets in the field, the electromotive force is entirely due to variation of electric potential, and we shall have (§ 65)

$$\mathrm{P} = -\frac{d\Psi}{dx}, \quad \mathrm{Q} = -\frac{d\Psi}{dy}, \quad \mathrm{R} = -\frac{d\Psi}{dz}.$$

Integrating by parts the expression (I) for the energy due to electric displacement, and remembering that P, Q, R vanish at an infinite distance, it becomes

$$\tfrac{1}{2}\Sigma\left\{\Psi\left(\frac{df}{dx} + \frac{dg}{dy} + \frac{dh}{dz}\right)\right\}d\mathrm{V},$$

or by the equation of Free Electricity (G), p. 485,

$$-\tfrac{1}{2}\Sigma(\Psi e)d\mathrm{V}.$$

By the same demonstration as was used in the case of the mechanical action on a magnet, it may be shown that the mechanical force on a small body containing a quantity e_2 of free electricity placed in a field whose potential arising from other electrified bodies is Ψ_1, has for components

$$
\left.
\begin{aligned}
X &= e_2 \frac{d\Psi_1}{dx} = -P_1 e_2, \\
Y &= e_2 \frac{d\Psi_1}{dy} = -Q_1 e_2, \\
Z &= e_2 \frac{d\Psi_1}{dz} = -R_1 e_2.
\end{aligned}
\right\} \quad \dots \dots \dots \dots \text{(D)}
$$

So that an electrified body is urged in the direction of the electromotive force with a force equal to the product of the quantity of free electricity and the electromotive force.

If the electrification of the field arises from the presence of a small electrified body containing e_1 of free electrity, the only solution of Ψ_1 is

$$
\Psi_1 = \frac{k}{4\pi} \frac{e_1}{r}, \quad \dots \dots \dots \dots \dots \text{(43)}
$$

where r is the distance from the electrified body.

The repulsion between two electrified bodies e_1, e_2 is therefore

$$
e_2 \frac{d\Psi_1}{dr} = \frac{k}{4\pi} \frac{e_1 e_2}{r^2}. \quad \dots \dots \dots \dots \text{(44)}
$$

Measurement of Electrical Phenomena by Electrostatic Effects.

(80) The quantities with which we have had to do have been hitherto expressed in terms of the Electromagnetic System of measurement, which is founded on the mechanical action between currents. The electrostatic system of measurement is founded on the mechanical action between electrified bodies, and is independent of, and incompatible with, the electromagnetic system; so that the units of the different kinds of quantity have different values according to the system we adopt, and to pass from the one system to the other, a reduction of all the quantities is required.

According to the electrostatic system, the repulsion between two small bodies charged with quantities η_1, η_2 of electricity is

$$
\frac{\eta_1 \eta_2}{r^2},
$$

where r is the distance between them.

Let the relation of the two systems be such that one electromagnetic unit of electricity contains v electrostatic units; then $\eta_1 = v e_1$ and $\eta_2 = v e_2$, and this repulsion becomes

$$
v^2 \frac{e_1 e_2}{r^2} = \frac{k}{4\pi} \frac{e_1 e_2}{r^2} \text{ by equation (44)}, \quad \dots \dots \quad \dots \dots \text{(45)}
$$

whence k, the coefficient of "electric elasticity" in the medium in which the experiments are made, i.e. common air, is related to v, the number of electrostatic units in one electromagnetic unit, by the equation

$$
k = 4\pi v^2. \quad \dots \dots \dots \dots \dots \text{(46)}
$$

The quantity v may be determined by experiment in several ways. According to the experiments of MM. WEBER and KOHLRAUSCH,

$$v=3!0,740,000 \text{ metres per second.}$$

(81) It appears from this investigation, that if we assume that the medium which constitutes the electromagnetic field is, when dielectric, capable of receiving in every part of it an electric polarization, in which the opposite sides of every element into which we may conceive the medium divided are oppositely electrified, and if we also assume that this polarization or electric displacement is proportional to the electromotive force which produces or maintains it, then we can show that electrified bodies in a dielectric medium will act on one another with forces obeying the same laws as are established by experiment.

The energy, by the expenditure of which electrical attractions and repulsions are produced, we suppose to be stored up in the dielectric medium which surrounds the electrified bodies, and not on the surface of those bodies themselves, which on our theory are merely the bounding surfaces of the air or other dielectric in which the true springs of action are to be sought.

Note on the Attraction of Gravitation.

(82) After tracing to the action of the surrounding medium both the magnetic and the electric attractions and repulsions, and finding them to depend on the inverse square of the distance, we are naturally led to inquire whether the attraction of gravitation, which follows the same law of the distance, is not also traceable to the action of a surrounding medium.

Gravitation differs from magnetism and electricity in this; that the bodies concerned are all of the same kind, instead of being of opposite signs, like magnetic poles and electrified bodies, and that the force between these bodies is an attraction and not a repulsion, as is the case between like electric and magnetic bodies.

The lines of gravitating force near two dense bodies are exactly of the same form as the lines of magnetic force near two poles of the same name; but whereas the poles are repelled, the bodies are attracted.   Let E be the intrinsic energy of the field surrounding two gravitating bodies M_1, M_2, and let E' be the intrinsic energy of the field surrounding two magnetic poles m_1, m_2, equal in numerical value to M_1, M_2, and let X be the gravitating force acting during the displacement δx, and X' the magnetic force,

$$X\delta x=\delta E, \qquad X'\delta x=\delta E';$$

now X and X' are equal in numerical value, but of opposite signs; so that

$$\delta E=-\delta E',$$

or

$$E=C-E'$$

$$=C-\Sigma \frac{1}{8\pi}(\alpha^2+\beta^2+\gamma^2)dV,$$

where α, β, γ are the components of magnetic intensity. If R be the resultant gravitating force, and R' the resultant magnetic force at a corresponding part of the field,

Hence
$$R = -R', \quad \text{and} \quad \alpha^2 + \beta^2 + \gamma^2 = R^2 = R'^2.$$

$$E = C - \Sigma \frac{1}{8\pi} R^2 dV. \quad . \quad . \quad . \quad . \quad . \quad . \quad . \quad . \quad . \quad . \quad . \quad (47)$$

The intrinsic energy of the field of gravitation must therefore be less wherever there is a resultant gravitating force.

As energy is essentially positive, it is impossible for any part of space to have negative intrinsic energy. Hence those parts of space in which there is no resultant force, such as the points of equilibrium in the space between the different bodies of a system, and within the substance of each body, must have an intrinsic energy per unit of volume greater than

$$\frac{1}{8\pi} R^2,$$

where R is the greatest possible value of the intensity of gravitating force in any part of the universe.

The assumption, therefore, that gravitation arises from the action of the surrounding medium in the way pointed out, leads to the conclusion that every part of this medium possesses, when undisturbed, an enormous intrinsic energy, and that the presence of dense bodies influences the medium so as to diminish this energy wherever there is a resultant attraction.

As I am unable to understand in what way a medium can possess such properties, I cannot go any further in this direction in searching for the cause of gravitation.

PART V.—THEORY OF CONDENSERS.

Capacity of a Condenser.

(83) The simplest form of condenser consists of a uniform layer of insulating matter bounded by two conducting surfaces, and its capacity is measured by the quantity of electricity on either surface when the difference of potentials is unity.

Let S be the area of either surface, a the thickness of the dielectric, and k its coefficient of electric elasticity; then on one side of the condenser the potential is Ψ_1, and on the other side $\Psi_1 + 1$, and within its substance

$$\frac{d\Psi}{dx} = \frac{1}{a} = kf. \quad . \quad . \quad . \quad . \quad . \quad . \quad . \quad . \quad . \quad (48)$$

Since $\frac{d\Psi}{dx}$ and therefore f is zero outside the condenser, the quantity of electricity on its first surface $= -Sf$, and on the second $+Sf$. The capacity of the condenser is therefore $Sf = \frac{S}{ak}$ in electromagnetic measure.

3 x 2

Specific Capacity of Electric Induction (D).

(84) If the dielectric of the condenser be air, then its capacity in electrostatic measure is $\frac{S}{4\pi a}$ (neglecting corrections arising from the conditions to be fulfilled at the edges). If the dielectric have a capacity whose ratio to that of air is D, then the capacity of the condenser will be $\frac{DS}{4\pi a}$.

Hence
$$D = \frac{k_0}{k}, \quad \ldots \ldots \ldots \ldots \ldots \ldots \quad (49)$$

where k_0 is the value of k in air, which is taken for unity.

Electric Absorption.

(85) When the dielectric of which the condenser is formed is not a perfect insulator, the phenomena of conduction are combined with those of electric displacement. The condenser, when left charged, gradually loses its charge, and in some cases, after being discharged completely, it gradually acquires a new charge of the same sign as the original charge, and this finally disappears. These phenomena have been described by Professor FARADAY (Experimental Researches, Series XI.) and by Mr. F. JENKIN (Report of Committee of Board of Trade on Submarine Cables), and may be classed under the name of "Electric Absorption."

(86) We shall take the case of a condenser composed of any number of parallel layers of different materials. If a constant difference of potentials between its extreme surfaces is kept up for a sufficient time till a condition of permanent steady flow of electricity is established, then each bounding surface will have a charge of electricity depending on the nature of the substances on each side of it. If the extreme surfaces be now discharged, these internal charges will gradually be dissipated, and a certain charge may reappear on the extreme surfaces if they are insulated, or, if they are connected by a conductor, a certain quantity of electricity may be urged through the conductor during the reestablishment of equilibrium.

Let the thickness of the several layers of the condenser be a_1, a_2, &c.

Let the values of k for these layers be respectively k_1, k_2, k_3, and let

$$a_1 k_2 + a_2 k_2 + \&c. = ak, \quad \ldots \ldots \ldots \ldots \quad (50)$$

where k is the "electric elasticity" of air, and a is the thickness of an equivalent condenser of air.

Let the resistances of the layers be respectively r_1, r_2, &c., and let $r_1 + r_2 + \&c. = r$ be the resistance of the whole condenser, to a steady current through it per unit of surface.

Let the electric displacement in each layer be f_1, f_2, &c.

Let the electric current in each layer be p_1, p_2, &c.

Let the potential on the first surface be Ψ_1, and the electricity per unit of surface e_1.

Let the corresponding quantities at the boundary of the first and second surface be Ψ_2 and e_2, and so on. Then by equations (G) and (H),

$$e_1 = -f_1, \qquad \frac{de_1}{dt} = -p_1,$$

$$e_2 = f_1 - f_2, \qquad \frac{de_2}{dt} = p_1 - p_2, \qquad \left. \right\} \quad \cdots \cdots \cdots \quad (51)$$

$$\&c. \qquad\qquad \&c.$$

But by equations (E) and (F),

$$\Psi_1 - \Psi_2 = a_1 k_1 f_1 = -r_1 p_1,$$

$$\Psi_2 - \Psi_3 = a_2 k_2 f_2 = -r_2 p_2, \qquad \left. \right\} \quad \cdots \cdots \cdots \quad (52)$$

$$\&c. \qquad \&c. \qquad \&c.$$

After the electromotive force has been kept up for a sufficient time the current becomes the same in each layer, and

$$p_1 = p_2 = \&c. = p = \frac{\Psi}{r},$$

where Ψ is the total difference of potentials between the extreme layers. We have then

$$f_1 = -\frac{\Psi}{r} \frac{r_1}{a_1 k_1}, \qquad f_2 = -\frac{\Psi}{r} \frac{r_2}{a_2 k_2}, \&c. \qquad \left. \right\}$$

and

$$\qquad\qquad\qquad\qquad\qquad\qquad\qquad\qquad\qquad \cdots \cdots \cdots \quad (53)$$

$$e_1 = \frac{\Psi}{r} \frac{r_1}{a_1 k_1}, \qquad e_2 = \frac{\Psi}{r}\left(\frac{r_2}{a_2 k_2} - \frac{r_1}{a k_1} \right), \&c. \qquad \left. \right\}$$

These are the quantities of electricity on the different surfaces.

(87) Now let the condenser be discharged by connecting the extreme surfaces through a perfect conductor so that their potentials are instantly rendered equal, then the electricity on the extreme surfaces will be altered, but that on the internal surfaces will not have time to escape. The total difference of potentials is now

$$\Psi' = a_1 k_1 e_1' + a_2 k_2 (e_1' + e_2) + a_3 k_3 (e_1' + e_2 + e_3), \&c. = 0, \quad \cdots \cdots \quad (54)$$

whence if e_1' is what e_1 becomes at the instant of discharge,

$$e_1' = \frac{\Psi}{r} \frac{r_1}{a_1 k_1} - \frac{\Psi}{ak} = e_1 - \frac{\Psi}{ak}. \quad \cdots \cdots \cdots \cdots \quad (55)$$

The instantaneous discharge is therefore $\frac{\Psi}{ak}$, or the quantity which would be discharged by a condenser of air of the equivalent thickness a, and it is unaffected by the want of perfect insulation.

(88) Now let us suppose the connexion between the extreme surfaces broken, and the condenser left to itself, and let us consider the gradual dissipation of the internal charges. Let Ψ' be the difference of potential of the extreme surfaces at any time t; then

$$\Psi' = a_1 k_1 f_1 + a_2 k_2 f_2 + \&c.; \quad \cdots \cdots \cdots \cdots \quad (56)$$

but

$$a_1 k_1 f_1 = -r_1 \frac{df_1}{dt},$$

$$a_2 k_2 f_2 = -r_2 \frac{df_2}{dt}.$$

Hence $f_1 = A_1 e^{-\frac{a_1 k_1}{r_1} t}$, $f_2 = A_2 e^{-\frac{a_2 k_2}{r_2} t}$, &c. ; and by referring to the values of e_1', e_2, &c., we find

$$A_1 = \frac{\Psi}{r} \frac{r_1}{a_1 k_1} - \frac{\Psi}{ak},$$

$$A_2 = \frac{\Psi}{r} \frac{r_2}{a_2 k_2} - \frac{\Psi}{ak}, \qquad \qquad \cdot \quad \cdot \quad \cdot \quad (57)$$

&c. ;

so that we find for the difference of extreme potentials at any time,

$$\Psi' = \Psi \left\{ \left(\frac{r_1}{r} - \frac{a_1 k_1}{ak} \right) e^{-\frac{a_1 k_1}{r_1} t} + \left(\frac{r_2}{r} - \frac{a_2 k_2}{ak} \right) e^{-\frac{a_2 k_2}{r_2} t} + \&c. \right\}. \quad \cdot \quad \cdot \quad \cdot \quad (58)$$

(89) It appears from this result that if all the layers are made of the same sub-stance, Ψ' will be zero always. If they are of different substances, the order in which they are placed is indifferent, and the effect will be the same whether each substance consists of one layer, or is divided into any number of thin layers and arranged in any order among thin layers of the other substances. Any substance, therefore, the parts of which are not mathematically homogeneous, though they may be apparently so, may exhibit phenomena of absorption. Also, since the order of magnitude of the coefficients is the same as that of the indices, the value of Ψ' can never change sign, but must start from zero, become positive, and finally disappear.

(90) Let us next consider the total amount of electricity which would pass from the first surface to the second, if the condenser, after being thoroughly saturated by the current and then discharged, has its extreme surfaces connected by a conductor of resistance R. Let p be the current in this conductor; then, during the discharge,

$$\Psi' = p_1 r_1 + p_2 r_2 + \&c. = pR. \quad \cdot \quad \cdot \quad \cdot \quad \cdot \quad \cdot \quad \cdot \quad (59)$$

Integrating with respect to the time, and calling q_1, q_2, q the quantities of electricity which traverse the different conductors,

$$q_1 r_1 + q_2 r_2 + \&c. = qR. \quad \cdot \quad \cdot \quad \cdot \quad \cdot \quad \cdot \quad \cdot \quad (60)$$

The quantities of electricity on the several surfaces will be

$$e_1' - q - q_1,$$
$$e_2 + q_1 - q_2,$$
&c. ;

and since at last all these quantities vanish, we find

$$q_1 = e_1' - q,$$
$$q_2 = e_1' + e_2 - q ;$$

whence

$$qR = \frac{\Psi}{r} \left(\frac{r_1^2}{a_1 k_1} + \frac{r_2^2}{a_2 k_2} + \&c. \right) - \frac{\Psi r}{ak},$$

or

$$q = \frac{\Psi}{akrR} \left\{ a_1 k_1 a_2 k_2 \left(\frac{r_1}{a_1 k_1} - \frac{r_2}{a_2 k_2} \right)^2 + a_2 k_2 a_3 k_3 \left(\frac{r_2}{a_2 k_2} - \frac{r_3}{a_3 k_3} \right)^2 + \&c. \right\}, \quad \cdot \quad \cdot \quad (61)$$

a quantity essentially positive; so that, when the primary electrification is in one direction, the secondary discharge is always in the same direction as the primary discharge[*].

PART VI.—ELECTROMAGNETIC THEORY OF LIGHT.

(91) At the commencement of this paper we made use of the optical hypothesis of an elastic medium through which the vibrations of light are propagated, in order to show that we have warrantable grounds for seeking, in the same medium, the cause of other phenomena as well as those of light. We then examined electromagnetic phenomena, seeking for their explanation in the properties of the field which surrounds the electrified or magnetic bodies. In this way we arrived at certain equations expressing certain properties of the electromagnetic field. We now proceed to investigate whether these properties of that which constitutes the electromagnetic field, deduced from electromagnetic phenomena alone, are sufficient to explain the propagation of light through the same substance.

(92) Let us suppose that a plane wave whose direction cosines are l, m, n is propagated through the field with a velocity V. Then all the electromagnetic functions will be functions of

$$w = lx + my + nz - \text{V}t.$$

The equations of Magnetic Force (B), p. 482, will become.

$$\mu\alpha = m\frac{d\text{H}}{dw} - n\frac{d\text{G}}{dw},$$

$$\mu\beta = n\frac{d\text{F}}{dw} - l\frac{d\text{H}}{dw},$$

$$\mu\gamma = l\frac{d\text{G}}{dw} - m\frac{d\text{F}}{dw}.$$

If we multiply these equations respectively by l, m, n, and add, we find

$$l\mu\alpha + m\mu\beta + n\mu\gamma = 0, \quad \ldots \ldots \quad (62)$$

which shows that the direction of the magnetization must be in the plane of the wave.

(93) If we combine the equations of Magnetic Force (B) with those of Electric Currents (C), and put for brevity

$$\frac{d\text{F}}{dx} + \frac{d\text{G}}{dy} + \frac{d\text{H}}{dz} = \text{J}, \text{ and } \frac{d^2}{dx^2} + \frac{d^2}{dy^2} + \frac{d^2}{dz^2} = \nabla^2, \quad \ldots \ldots \quad (63)$$

$$
\left.
\begin{aligned}
4\pi\mu p' &= \frac{d\text{J}}{dx} - \nabla^2\text{F}, \\
4\pi\mu q' &= \frac{d\text{J}}{dy} - \nabla^2\text{G}, \\
4\pi\mu r' &= \frac{d\text{J}}{dz} - \nabla^2\text{H}.
\end{aligned}
\right\} \quad \ldots \ldots \quad (64)
$$

---

[*] Since this paper was communicated to the Royal Society, I have seen a paper by M. GAUGAIN in the Annales de Chimie for 1864, in which he has deduced the phenomena of electric absorption and secondary discharge from the theory of compound condensers.

If the medium in the field is a perfect dielectric there is no true conduction, and the currents p', q', r' are only variations in the electric displacement, or, by the equations of Total Currents (A),

$$p'=\frac{df}{dt}, \qquad q'=\frac{dg}{dt}, \qquad r'=\frac{dh}{dt}. \quad \ldots \ldots \ldots (65)$$

But these electric displacements are caused by electromotive forces, and by the equations of Electric Elasticity (E),

$$P=kf, \qquad Q=kg, \qquad R=kh. \quad \ldots \ldots \ldots (66)$$

These electromotive forces are due to the variations either of the electromagnetic or the electrostatic functions, as there is no motion of conductors in the field; so that the equations of electromotive force (D) are

$$\left. \begin{aligned} P &= -\frac{dF}{dt}-\frac{d\Psi}{dx}, \\ Q &= -\frac{dG}{dt}-\frac{d\Psi}{dy}, \\ R &= -\frac{dH}{dt}-\frac{d\Psi}{dz}. \end{aligned} \right\} \quad \ldots \ldots \ldots (67)$$

(94) Combining these equations, we obtain the following:—

$$\left. \begin{aligned} k\left(\frac{dJ}{dx}-\nabla^2 F\right)+4\pi\mu\left(\frac{d^2 F}{dt^2}+\frac{d^2\Psi}{dxdt}\right) &= 0, \\ k\left(\frac{dJ}{dy}-\nabla^2 G\right)+4\pi\mu\left(\frac{d^2 G}{dt^2}+\frac{d^2\Psi}{dydt}\right) &= 0, \\ k\left(\frac{dJ}{dz}-\nabla^2 H\right)+4\pi\mu\left(\frac{d^2 H}{dt^2}+\frac{d^2\Psi}{dzdt}\right) &= 0. \end{aligned} \right\} \quad \ldots \ldots (68)$$

If we differentiate the third of these equations with respect to y, and the second with respect to z, and subtract, J and Ψ disappear, and by remembering the equations (B) of magnetic force, the results may be written

$$\left. \begin{aligned} k\nabla^2\mu\alpha &= 4\pi\mu\frac{d^2}{dt^2}\mu\alpha, \\ k\nabla^2\mu\beta &= 4\pi\mu\frac{d^2}{dt^2}\mu\beta, \\ k\nabla^2\mu\gamma &= 4\pi\mu\frac{d^2}{d^2t}\mu\gamma. \end{aligned} \right\} \quad \ldots \ldots \ldots (69)$$

(95) If we assume that α, β, γ are functions of $lx+my+nz-Vt=w$, the first equation becomes

$$k\mu\frac{d^2\alpha}{dw^2}=4\pi\mu^2 V^2\frac{d^2\alpha}{dw^2}, \quad \ldots \ldots \ldots (70)$$

or

$$V=\pm\sqrt{\frac{k}{4\pi\mu}}. \quad \ldots \ldots \ldots \ldots (71)$$

The other equations give the same value for V, so that the wave is propagated in either direction with a velocity V.

This wave consists entirely of magnetic disturbances, the direction of magnetization being in the plane of the wave. No magnetic disturbance whose direction of magnetization is not in the plane of the wave can be propagated as a plane wave at all.

Hence magnetic disturbances propagated through the electromagnetic field agree with light in this, that the disturbance at any point is transverse to the direction of propagation, and such waves may have all the properties of polarized light.

(96) The only medium in which experiments have been made to determine the value of k is air, in which $\mu=1$, and therefore, by equation (46),

$$V=v. \qquad \ldots \ldots \ldots \ldots \qquad (72)$$

By the electromagnetic experiments of MM. WEBER and KOHLRAUSCH [*],

$$v=310,740,000 \text{ metres per second}$$

is the number of electrostatic units in one electromagnetic unit of electricity, and this, according to our result, should be equal to the velocity of light in air or vacuum.

The velocity of light in air, by M. FIZEAU's[†] experiments, is

$$V=314,858,000:$$

according to the more accurate experiments of M. FOUCAULT [‡],

$$V=298,000,000.$$

The velocity of light in the space surrounding the earth, deduced from the coefficient of aberration and the received value of the radius of the earth's orbit, is

$$V=308,000,000.$$

(97) Hence the velocity of light deduced from experiment agrees sufficiently well with the value of v deduced from the only set of experiments we as yet possess. The value of v was determined by measuring the electromotive force with which a condenser of known capacity was charged, and then discharging the condenser through a galvanometer, so as to measure the quantity of electricity in it in electromagnetic measure. The only use made of light in the experiment was to see the instruments. The value of V found by M. FOUCAULT was obtained by determining the angle through which a revolving mirror turned, while the light reflected from it went and returned along a measured course. No use whatever was made of electricity or magnetism.

The agreement of the results seems to show that light and magnetism are affections of the same substance, and that light is an electromagnetic disturbance propagated through the field according to electromagnetic laws.

(98) Let us now go back upon the equations in (94), in which the quantities J and Ψ occur, to see whether any other kind of disturbance can be propagated through the medium depending on these quantities which disappeared from the final equations.

* Leipzig Transactions, vol. v. (1857), p. 260, or POGGENDORFF's 'Annalen,' Aug. 1856, p. 10.
† Comptes Rendus, vol. xxix. (1849), p. 90.   ‡ Ibid. vol. lv. (1862), pp. 501, 792.

If we determine χ from the equation

$$\nabla^2\chi = \frac{d^2\chi}{dx^2} + \frac{d^2\chi}{dy^2} + \frac{d^2\chi}{dz^2} = J, \quad \ldots \ldots \ldots (73)$$

and F', G', H' from the equations

$$F' = F - \frac{d\chi}{dx}, \quad G' = G - \frac{d\chi}{dy}, \quad H' = H - \frac{d\chi}{dz}, \quad \ldots (74)$$

then

$$\frac{dF'}{dx} + \frac{dG'}{dy} + \frac{dH'}{dz} = 0, \quad \ldots \ldots \ldots (75)$$

and the equations in (94) become of the form

$$k\nabla^2F' = 4\pi\mu\left(\frac{d^2F'}{dt^2} + \frac{d}{dxdt}\left(\Psi + \frac{d\chi}{dt}\right)\right). \quad \ldots \ldots (76)$$

Differentiating the three equations with respect to x, y, and z, and adding, we find that

$$\Psi = -\frac{d\chi}{dt} + \varphi(x, y, z), \quad \ldots \ldots \ldots (77)$$

and that

$$k\nabla^2F' = 4\pi\mu\frac{d^2F'}{dt^2},$$
$$k\nabla^2G' = 4\pi\mu\frac{d^2G'}{dt^2}, \quad \left.\right\} \quad \ldots \ldots \ldots (78)$$
$$k\nabla^2H' = 4\pi\mu\frac{d^2H'}{dt^2}.$$

Hence the disturbances indicated by F', G', H' are propagated with the velocity $V = \sqrt{\frac{k}{4\pi\mu}}$ through the field; and since

$$\frac{dF'}{dx} + \frac{dG'}{dy} + \frac{dH'}{dx} = 0,$$

the resultant of these disturbances is in the plane of the wave.

(99) The remaining part of the total disturbances F, G, H being the part depending on χ, is subject to no condition except that expressed in the equation

$$\frac{d\Psi}{dt} + \frac{d^2\chi}{dt^2} = 0.$$

If we perform the operation ∇^2 on this equation, it becomes

$$ke = \frac{dJ}{dt} - k\nabla^2\varphi(x, y, z). \quad \ldots \ldots \ldots (79)$$

Since the medium is a perfect insulator, e, the free electricity, is immoveable, and therefore $\frac{dJ}{dt}$ is a function of x, y, z, and the value of J is either constant or zero, or uniformly increasing or diminishing with the time; so that no disturbance depending on J can be propagated as a wave.

(100) The equations of the electromagnetic field, deduced from purely experimental evidence, show that transversal vibrations only can be propagated. . If we were to go beyond our experimental knowledge and to assign a definite density to a substance which

we should call the electric fluid, and select either vitreous or resinous electricity as the representative of that fluid, then we might have normal vibrations propagated with a velocity depending on this density. We have, however, no evidence as to the density of electricity, as we do not even know whether to consider vitreous electricity as a substance or as the absence of a substance.

Hence electromagnetic science leads to exactly the same conclusions as optical science with respect to the direction of the disturbances which can be propagated through the field; both affirm the propagation of transverse vibrations, and both give the same velocity of propagation. On the other hand, both sciences are at a loss when called on to affirm or deny the existence of normal vibrations.

Relation between the Index of Refraction and the Electromagnetic Character of the substance.

(101) The velocity of light in a medium, according to the Undulatory Theory, is

$$\frac{1}{i}V_0,$$

where i is the index of refraction and V_0 is the velocity in vacuum. The velocity, according to the Electromagnetic Theory, is

$$\sqrt{\frac{k}{4\pi\mu}},$$

where, by equations (49) and (71), $k=\frac{1}{D}k_0$, and $k_0=4\pi V_0^2$.

Hence
$$D=\frac{i^2}{\mu}, \quad \cdots \cdots \cdots \quad (80)$$

or the Specific Inductive Capacity is equal to the square of the index of refraction, divided by the coefficient of magnetic induction.

Propagation of Electromagnetic Disturbances in a Crystallized Medium.

(102) Let us now calculate the conditions of propagation of a plane wave in a medium for which the values of k and μ are different in different directions. As we, do not propose to give a complete investigation of the question in the present imperfect state of the theory as extended to disturbances of short period, we shall assume that the axes of magnetic induction coincide in direction with those of electric elasticity.

(103) Let the values of the magnetic coefficient for the three axes be λ, μ, ν, then the equations of magnetic force (B) become

$$\left.\begin{array}{l} \lambda\alpha = \dfrac{dH}{dy} - \dfrac{dG}{dz}, \\[2mm] \mu\beta = \dfrac{dF}{dz} - \dfrac{dH}{dx}, \\[2mm] \nu\gamma = \dfrac{dG}{dx} - \dfrac{dF}{dy}. \end{array}\right\} \quad \cdots \cdots \cdots \quad (81)$$

3 Y 2

The equations of electric currents (C) remain as before.

The equations of electric elasticity (E) will be

$$\left.\begin{array}{l} P = 4\pi a^2 f, \\ Q = 4\pi b^2 g, \\ R = 4\pi c^2 h, \end{array}\right\} \quad \dots \dots \dots \quad (82)$$

where $4\pi a^2$, $4\pi b^2$, and $4\pi c^2$ are the values of k for the axes of x, y, z.

Combining these equations with (A) and (D), we get equations of the form

$$\frac{1}{\mu\nu}\left(\lambda\frac{d^2 F}{dx^2} + \mu\frac{d^2 F}{dy^2} + \nu\frac{d^2 F}{dz^2}\right) - \frac{1}{\mu\nu}\frac{d}{dx}\left(\lambda\frac{dF}{dx} + \mu\frac{dG}{dy} + \nu\frac{dH}{dz}\right) = \frac{1}{a^2}\left(\frac{d^2 F}{dt^2} + \frac{d^2 \Psi}{dx\,dt}\right). \quad (83)$$

(104) If l, m, n are the direction-cosines of the wave, and V its velocity, and if

$$lx + my + nz - Vt = w, \quad \dots \dots \dots \quad (84)$$

then F, G, H, and Ψ will be functions of w; and if we put F', G', H', Ψ' for the second differentials of these quantities with respect to w, the equations will be

$$\left.\begin{array}{l} \left(V^2 - a^2\left(\dfrac{m^2}{\nu} + \dfrac{n^2}{\mu}\right)\right)F' + \dfrac{a^2 lm}{\nu}G' + \dfrac{a^2 ln}{\mu}H' - lV\Psi' = 0, \\[2mm] \left(V^2 - b^2\left(\dfrac{n^2}{\lambda} + \dfrac{l^2}{\nu}\right)\right)G' + \dfrac{b^2 mn}{\lambda}H' + \dfrac{b^2 ml}{\nu}F' - mV\Psi' = 0, \\[2mm] \left(V^2 - c^2\left(\dfrac{l^2}{\mu} + \dfrac{m^2}{\lambda}\right)\right)H' + \dfrac{c^2 nl}{\mu}F' + \dfrac{c^2 nm}{\lambda}G' - nV\Psi' = 0. \end{array}\right\} \quad \dots \quad (85)$$

If we now put

$$\left.\begin{array}{l} V^4 - V^2\dfrac{1}{\lambda\mu\nu}\left\{l^2\lambda(b^2\mu + c^2\nu) + m^2\mu(c^2\nu + a^2\lambda) + n^2\nu(a^2\lambda + b^2\mu)\right\} \\[2mm] \qquad + \dfrac{a^2 b^2 c^2}{\lambda\mu\nu}\left(\dfrac{l^2}{a^2} + \dfrac{m^2}{b^2} + \dfrac{n^2}{c^2}\right)(l^2\lambda + m^2\mu + n^2\nu) = U, \end{array}\right\} \quad \dots \quad (86)$$

we shall find

$$F'V^2 U - l\Psi'VU = 0, \quad \dots \dots \dots \quad (87)$$

with two similar equations for G' and H'. Hence either

$$V = 0, \quad \dots \dots \dots \dots \dots \quad (88)$$

$$U = 0, \quad \dots \dots \dots \dots \dots \quad (89)$$

or

$$VF' = l\Psi', \quad VG' = m\Psi' \text{ and } VH' = n\Psi'. \quad \dots \quad (90)$$

The third supposition indicates that the resultant of F', G', H' is in the direction normal to the plane of the wave; but the equations do not indicate that such a disturbance, if possible, could be propagated, as we have no other relation between Ψ' and F', G', H'.

The solution $V = 0$ refers to a case in which there is no propagation.

The solution $U = 0$ gives two values for V^2 corresponding to values of F', G', H', which are given by the equations

$$\frac{l}{a^2}F' + \frac{m}{b^2}G' + \frac{n}{c^2}H' = 0, \quad \dots \dots \dots \dots \dots \quad (91)$$

$$\frac{a^2l\lambda}{F'}(b^2\mu - c^2\nu) + \frac{b^2m\mu}{G'}(c^2\nu - a^2\lambda) + \frac{c^2n\nu}{H'}(a^2\lambda - b^2\mu) = 0, \quad \dots \dots \quad (92)$$

(105) The velocities along the axes are as follows:—

Direction of propagation		x	y	z
	x		$\dfrac{a^2}{\nu}$	$\dfrac{a^2}{\mu}$
Direction of the electric displacements	y	$\dfrac{b^2}{\nu}$		$\dfrac{b^2}{\lambda}$
	z	$\dfrac{c^2}{\mu}$	$\dfrac{c^2}{\lambda}$	

Now we know that in each principal plane of a crystal the ray polarized in that plane obeys the ordinary law of refraction, and therefore its velocity is the same in whatever direction in that plane it is propagated.

If polarized light consists of electromagnetic disturbances in which the electric displacement is in the plane of polarization, then

$$a^2 = b^2 = c^2. \quad \dots \dots \dots \dots \dots \quad (93)$$

If, on the contrary, the electric displacements are perpendicular to the plane of polarization,

$$\lambda = \mu = \nu. \quad \dots \dots \dots \dots \dots \quad (94)$$

We know, from the magnetic experiments of FARADAY, PLÜCKER, &c., that in many crystals λ, μ, ν are unequal.

The experiments of KNOBLAUCH* on electric induction through crystals seem to show that a, b and c, may be different.

The inequality, however, of λ, μ, ν is so small that great magnetic forces are required to indicate their difference, and the differences do not seem of sufficient magnitude to account for the double refraction of the crystals.

On the other hand, experiments on electric induction are liable to error on account of minute flaws, or portions of conducting matter in the crystal.

Further experiments on the magnetic and dielectric properties of crystals are required before we can decide whether the relation of these bodies to magnetic and electric forces is the same, when these forces are permanent as when they are alternating with the rapidity of the vibrations of light.

* Philosophical Magazine, 1852.

Relation between Electric Resistance and Transparency.

(106) If the medium, instead of being a perfect insulator, is a conductor whose resistance per unit of volume is ϱ, then there will be not only electric displacements, but true currents of conduction in which electrical energy is transformed into heat, and the undulation is thereby weakened. To determine the coefficient of absorption, let us investigate the propagation along the axis of x of the transverse disturbance G.

By the former equations

$$\frac{d^2G}{dx^2} = -4\pi\mu(q')$$

$$= -4\pi\mu\left(\frac{df}{dt}+q\right) \text{ by (A)},$$

$$\frac{d^2G}{dx^2} = +4\pi\mu\left(\frac{1}{k}\frac{d^2G}{dt^2} - \frac{1}{\varrho}\frac{dG}{dt}\right) \text{ by (E) and (F).} \quad \ldots \ldots \quad (95)$$

If G is of the form

$$G = e^{-px}\cos(qx+nt), \quad \ldots \ldots \ldots \ldots \ldots \quad (96)$$

we find that

$$p = \frac{2\pi\mu}{\varrho}\frac{n}{q} = \frac{2\pi\mu}{\varrho}\frac{V}{i}, \quad \ldots \ldots \ldots \ldots \ldots \quad (97)$$

where V is the velocity of light in air, and i is the index of refraction. The proportion of incident light transmitted through the thickness x is

$$e^{-2px}. \quad \ldots \ldots \ldots \ldots \ldots \quad (98)$$

Let R be the resistance in electromagnetic measure of a plate of the substance whose thickness is x, breadth b, and length l, then

$$R = \frac{l\varrho}{bx},$$

$$2px = 4\pi\mu\frac{V}{i}\frac{l}{bR}. \quad \ldots \ldots \ldots \ldots \quad (99)$$

(107) Most transparent solid bodies are good insulators, whereas all good conductors are very opaque.

Electrolytes allow a current to pass easily and yet are often very transparent. We may suppose, however, that in the rapidly alternating vibrations of light, the electromotive forces act for so short a time that they are unable to effect a complete separation between the particles in combination, so that when the force is reversed the particles oscillate into their former position without loss of energy.

Gold, silver, and platinum are good conductors, and yet when reduced to sufficiently thin plates they allow light to pass through them. If the resistance of gold is the same for electromotive forces of short period as for those with which we make experiments, the amount of light which passes through a piece of gold-leaf, of which the resistance was determined by Mr. C. HOCKIN, would be only 10^{-50} of the incident light, a totally imperceptible quantity. I find that between $\frac{1}{500}$ and $\frac{1}{1000}$ of green light gets through such gold-leaf. Much of this is transmitted through holes and cracks; there is enough, however, transmitted through the gold itself to give a strong green hue to the transmitted light. This result cannot be reconciled with the electromagnetic theory of light, unless we suppose that there is less loss of energy when the electromotive forces are reversed with the rapidity of the vibrations of light than when they act for sensible times, as in our experiments.

Absolute Values of the Electromotive and Magnetic Forces called into play in the Propagation of Light.

(108) If the equation of propagation of light is

$$F = A \cos \frac{2\pi}{\lambda}(z - Vt),$$

the electromotive force will be

$$P = -A \frac{2\pi}{\lambda} V \sin \frac{2\pi}{\lambda}(z - Vt);$$

and the energy per unit of volume will be

$$\frac{P^2}{8\pi\mu V^2},$$

where P represents the greatest value of the electromotive force. Half of this consists of magnetic and half of electric energy.

The energy passing through a unit of area is

$$W = \frac{P^2}{8\pi\mu V};$$

so that

$$P = \sqrt{8\pi\mu VW},$$

where V is the velocity of light, and W is the energy communicated to unit of area by the light in a second.

According to POUILLET's data, as calculated by Professor W. THOMSON [*], the mechanical value of direct sunlight at the Earth is

83·4 foot-pounds per second per square foot.

This gives the maximum value of P in direct sunlight at the Earth's distance from the Sun,

P = 60,000,000,

or about 600 DANIELL's cells per metre.

At the Sun's surface the value of P would be about

13,000 DANIELL's cells per metre.

At the Earth the maximum magnetic force would be ·193 [†].

At the Sun it would be 4·13.

These electromotive and magnetic forces must be conceived to be reversed twice in every vibration of light; that is, more than a thousand million million times in a second.

---

[*] Transactions of the Royal Society of Edinburgh, 1854 ("Mechanical Energies of the Solar System").

[†] The horizontal magnetic force at Kew is about 1·76 in metrical units.

PART VII.—CALCULATION OF THE COEFFICIENTS OF ELECTROMAGNETIC INDUCTION.

General Methods.

(109) The electromagnetic relations between two conducting circuits, A and B, depend upon a function M of their form and relative position, as has been already shown.

M may be calculated in several different ways, which must of course all lead to the same result.

First Method. M is the electromagnetic momentum of the circuit B when A carries a unit current, or

$$M = \int \left(F \frac{dx}{ds'} + G \frac{dy}{ds'} + H \frac{dz}{ds'} \right) ds',$$

where F, G, H are the components of electromagnetic momentum due to a unit current in A, and ds' is an element of length of B, and the integration is performed round the circuit of B.

To find F, G, H, we observe that by (B) and (C)

$$\frac{d^2 F}{dx^2} + \frac{d^2 F}{dy^2} + \frac{d^2 F}{dz^2} = -4\pi \mu p',$$

with corresponding equations for G and H, p', q', and r' being the components of the current in A.

Now if we consider only a single element ds of A, we shall have

$$p' = \frac{dx}{ds} ds, \qquad q' = \frac{dy}{ds} ds, \qquad r' = \frac{dz}{ds} ds,$$

and the solution of the equation gives

$$F = \frac{\mu}{\varrho} \frac{dx}{ds} ds, \qquad G = \frac{\mu}{\varrho} \frac{dy}{ds} ds, \qquad H = \frac{\mu}{\varrho} \frac{dz}{ds} ds,$$

where ϱ is the distance of any point from ds. Hence

$$M = \iint \frac{\mu}{\varrho} \left(\frac{dx}{ds} \frac{dx}{ds'} + \frac{dy}{ds} \frac{dy}{ds'} + \frac{dz}{ds} \frac{dz}{ds'} \right) ds ds'$$

$$= \iint \frac{\mu}{\varrho} \cos \theta \, ds ds',$$

where θ is the angle between the directions of the two elements ds, ds', and ϱ is the distance between them, and the integration is performed round both circuits.

In this method we confine our attention during integration to the two linear circuits alone.

(110) Second Method. M is the number of lines of magnetic force which pass through the circuit B when A carries a unit current, or

$$M = \Sigma(\mu \alpha l + \mu \beta m + \mu \gamma n) dS',$$

where $\mu \alpha$, $\mu \beta$, $\mu \gamma$ are the components of magnetic induction due to unit current in A,

S' is a surface bounded by the current B, and l, m, n are the direction-cosines of the normal to the surface, the integration being extended over the surface.

We may express this in the form

$$M = \mu \Sigma \frac{1}{\varrho^2} \sin \theta \sin \theta' \sin \varphi dS'ds,$$

where dS' is an element of the surface bounded by B, ds is an element of the circuit A, ϱ is the distance between them, θ and θ' are the angles between ϱ and ds and between ϱ and the normal to dS' respectively, and φ is the angle between the planes in which θ and θ' are measured. The integration is performed round the circuit A and over the surface bounded by B.

This method is most convenient in the case of circuits lying in one plane, in which case $\sin \theta = 1$, and $\sin \varphi = 1$.

111. Third Method. M is that part of the intrinsic magnetic energy of the whole field which depends on the product of the currents in the two circuits, each current being unity.

Let α, β, γ be the components of magnetic intensity at any point due to the first circuit, α', β', γ' the same for the second circuit; then the intrinsic energy of the element of volume dV of the field is

$$\frac{\mu}{8\pi}\left((\alpha+\alpha')^2 + (\beta+\beta')^2 + (\gamma+\gamma')^2\right)dV.$$

The part which depends on the product of the currents is

$$\frac{\mu}{4\pi}(\alpha\alpha' + \beta\beta' + \gamma\gamma')dV.$$

Hence if we know the magnetic intensities I and I' due to unit current in each circuit, we may obtain M by integrating

$$\frac{\mu}{4\pi}\Sigma\mu I \, I' \cos \theta dV$$

over all space, where θ is the angle between the directions of I and I'.

Application to a Coil.

(112) To find the coefficient (M) of mutual induction between two circular linear conductors in parallel planes, the distance between the curves being everywhere the same, and small compared with the radius of either.

If r be the distance between the curves, and a the radius of either, then when r is very small compared with a, we find by the second method, as a first approximation,

$$M = 4\pi a \left(\log_e \frac{8a}{r} - 2\right).$$

To approximate more closely to the value of M, let a and a_1 be the radii of the circles, and b the distance between their planes; then

$$r^2 = (a-a_1)^2 + b^2.$$

3 z

We obtain M by considering the following conditions:—

1st. M must fulfil the differential equation

$$\frac{d^2 M}{da^2} + \frac{d^2 M}{db^2} + \frac{1}{a}\frac{dM}{da} = 0.$$

This equation being true for any magnetic field symmetrical with respect to the common axis of the circles, cannot of itself lead to the determination of M as a function of a, a_1, and b. We therefore make use of other conditions.

2ndly. The value of M must remain the same when a and a_1 are exchanged.

3rdly. The first two terms of M must be the same as those given above.

M may thus be expanded in the following series:—

$$M = 4\pi a \log \frac{8a}{r}\left\{1 + \frac{1}{2}\frac{a-a_1}{a} + \frac{1}{16}\frac{3b^2 + (a_1 - a)^2}{a^2} - \frac{1}{32}\frac{(3b^2 + (a-a_1)^2)(a-a_1)}{a^3} + \&c.\right\}$$

$$- 4\pi a\left\{2 + \frac{1}{2}\frac{a-a_1}{a} + \frac{1}{16}\frac{b^2 - 3(a-a_1^2)}{a^2} - \frac{1}{48}\frac{(6b^2 - (a-a_1)^2)(a-a_1)}{a^3} + \&c.\right\}.$$

(113) We may apply this result to find the coefficient of self-induction (L) of a circular coil of wire whose section is small compared with the radius of the circle.

Let the section of the coil be a rectangle, the breadth in the plane of the circle being c, and the depth perpendicular to the plane of the circle being b.

Let the mean radius of the coil be a, and the number of windings n; then we find, by integrating,

$$L = \frac{n^2}{b^2 c^2}\iiiint M(xy\, x'y')dx\, dy\, dx'\, dy',$$

where $M(xy\, x'y')$ means the value of M for the two windings whose coordinates are xy and $x'y'$ respectively; and the integration is performed first with respect to x and y over the rectangular section, and then with respect to x' and y' over the same space.

$$L = 4\pi n^2 a\left\{\log_e\frac{8a}{r} + \frac{1}{12} - \frac{4}{3}\left(\theta - \frac{\pi}{4}\right)\cot 2\theta - \frac{\pi}{3}\cos 2\theta - \frac{1}{6}\cot^2\theta \log\cos\theta - \frac{1}{6}\tan^2\theta\log\sin\theta\right\}$$

$$+ \frac{\pi n^2 r^2}{24a}\left\{\log\frac{8a}{r}(2\sin^2\theta + 1) + 3\cdot 45 + 27\cdot 475\cos^2\theta - 3\cdot 2\left(\frac{\pi}{2} - \theta\right)\frac{\sin^3\theta}{\cos\theta} + \frac{1}{5}\frac{\cos^4\theta}{\sin^2\theta}\log\cos\theta\right.$$

$$\left. + \frac{13}{3}\frac{\sin^4\theta}{\cos^2\theta}\log\sin\theta\right\} + \&c.$$

Here $a=$ mean radius of the coil.

,, $r=$ diagonal of the rectangular section $=\sqrt{b^2 + c^2}$.

,, $\theta=$ angle between r and the plane of the circle.

,, $n=$ number of windings.

The logarithms are Napierian, and the angles are in circular measure.

In the experiments made by the Committee of the British Association for determining a standard of Electrical Resistance, a double coil was used, consisting of two nearly equal coils of rectangular section, placed parallel to each other, with a small interval between them.

The value of L for this coil was found in the following way.

The value of L was calculated by the preceding formula for six different cases, in which the rectangular section considered has always the same breadth, while the depth was

$$A, \ B, \ C, \quad A+B, \quad B+C, \quad A+B+C,$$

and $n=1$ in each case.

Calling the results

$$L(A), \quad L(B), \quad L(C), \ \&c.,$$

we calculate the coefficient of mutual induction M(AC) of the two coils thus,

$$2ACM(AC)=(A+B+C)^2L(A+B+C)-(A+B)^2L(A+B)-(B+C)^2L(B+C)+B^2L(B).$$

Then if n_1 is the number of windings in the coil A and n_2 in the coil B, the coefficient of self-induction of the two coils together is

$$L=n_1^2L(A)+2n_1n_2L(AC)+n_2^2L(B).$$

(114) These values of L are calculated on the supposition that the windings of the wire are evenly distributed so as to fill up exactly the whole section. This, however, is not the case, as the wire is generally circular and covered with insulating material. Hence the current in the wire is more concentrated than it would have been if it had been distributed uniformly over the section, and the currents in the neighbouring wires do not act on it exactly as such a uniform current would do.

The corrections arising from these considerations may be expressed as numerical quantities, by which we must multiply the length of the wire, and they are the same whatever be the form of the coil.

Let the distance between each wire and the next, on the supposition that they are arranged in square order, be D, and let the diameter of the wire be d, then the correction for diameter of wire is

$$+2\left(\log\frac{D}{d}+\frac{4}{3}\log 2+\frac{\pi}{3}-\frac{11}{6}\right).$$

The correction for the eight nearest wires is

$$+0{\cdot}0236.$$

For the sixteen in the next row

$$+0{\cdot}00083.$$

These corrections being multiplied by the length of wire and added to the former result, give the true value of L, considered as the measure of the potential of the coil on itself for unit current in the wire when that current has been established for some time, and is uniformly distributed through the section of the wire.

(115) But at the commencement of a current and during its variation the current is not uniform throughout the section of the wire, because the inductive action between different portions of the current tends to make the current stronger at one part of the section than at another. When a uniform electromotive force P arising from any cause

acts on a cylindrical wire of specific resistance ϱ, we have

$$p\varrho = P - \frac{dF}{dt},$$

where F is got from the equation

$$\frac{d^2F}{dr^2} + \frac{1}{r}\frac{dF}{dr} = -4\pi\mu p,$$

r being the distance from the axis of the cylinder.

Let one term of the value of F be of the form Tr^n, where T is a function of the time, then the term of p which produced it is of the form

$$-\frac{1}{4\pi\mu}n^2Tr^{n-2}.$$

Hence if we write

$$F = T + \frac{\mu\pi}{\varrho}\left(-P + \frac{dT}{dt}\right)r^2 + \overline{\frac{\mu\pi}{\varrho}}\Big|^2\frac{1}{1^2 \cdot 2^2}\frac{dT^2}{dt^2}r^4 + \&c.$$

$$p\varrho = \left(P + \frac{dT}{dt}\right) - \frac{\mu\pi}{\varrho}\frac{d^2T}{dt^2}r^2 - \overline{\frac{\mu\pi}{\varrho}}\Big|^2\frac{1}{1^2 \cdot 2^2}\frac{d^3T}{dt^3}r^4 - \&c.$$

The total counter current of self-induction at any point is

$$\int\left(\frac{P}{\varrho} - p\right)dt = \frac{1}{\varrho}T + \frac{\mu\pi}{\varrho^2}\frac{dT}{dt}r^2 + \frac{\mu^2\pi^2}{\varrho^3}\frac{1}{1^2 2^2}\frac{d^2T}{dt^2}r^4 + \&c.$$

from $t = 0$ to $t = \infty$.

When $t = 0$, $p = 0$, $\therefore \left(\frac{dT}{dt}\right)_0 = P$, $\left(\frac{d^2T}{dt^2}\right)_0 = 0$, &c.

When $t = \infty$, $p = \frac{P}{\varrho}$, $\therefore \left(\frac{dT}{dt}\right)_\infty = 0$, $\left(\frac{d^2T}{dt^2}\right)_\infty = 0$, &c.

$$\int_0^\infty\int_0^r 2\pi\left(\frac{P}{\varrho} - p\right)r\,dr\,dt = \frac{1}{\varrho}T\pi r^2 + \frac{1}{2}\frac{\mu\pi^2}{\varrho^2}\frac{dT}{dt}r^4 + \frac{\mu^2\pi^3}{\varrho^3}\frac{1}{1^2 \cdot 2^2 \cdot 3}\frac{d^2T}{dt^2}r^6 + \&c.$$

from $t = 0$ to $= \infty$.

When $t = 0$, $p = 0$ throughout the section, $\therefore \left(\frac{dT}{dt}\right)_0 = P$, $\left(\frac{d^2T}{dt^2}\right)_0 = 0$, &c.

When $t = \infty$, $p = 0$ throughout . . . . . $\therefore \left(\frac{dT}{dt}\right)_\infty = 0$, $\left(\frac{d^2T}{dt^2}\right)_\infty = 0$, &c.

Also if l be the length of the wire, and R its resistance,

$$R = \frac{\varrho l}{\pi r^2};$$

and if C be the current when established in the wire, $C = \frac{Pl}{R}$.

The total counter current may be written

$$\frac{l}{R}(T_\infty - T_0) - \frac{1}{2}\mu\frac{l}{R}C = -\frac{LC}{R} \text{ by } \S (35).$$

Now if the current instead of being variable from the centre to the circumference of the section of the wire had been the same throughout, the value of F would have been

$$F = T + \mu\gamma\left(1 - \frac{r^2}{r_0^2}\right),$$

where γ is the current in the wire at any instant, and the total countercurrent would have been

$$\int_0^\infty \int_0^r \frac{1}{\varrho} \frac{dF}{dt} 2\pi r\, dr = \frac{l}{R}(T_\infty - T_0) - \frac{3}{4}\mu\frac{l}{R}C = -\frac{l'C}{R}, \text{ say.}$$

Hence

$$L = L' - \tfrac{1}{4}\mu l,$$

or the value of L which must be used in calculating the self-induction of a wire for variable currents is less than that which is deduced from the supposition of the current being constant throughout the section of the wire by $\frac{1}{4}\mu l$, where l is the length of the wire, and μ is the coefficient of magnetic induction for the substance of the wire.

(116) The dimensions of the coil used by the Committee of the British Association in their experiments at King's College in 1864 were as follows:—

metre.

Mean radius	$= a = \cdot158194$
Depth of each coil	$= b = \cdot01608$
Breadth of each coil	$= c = \cdot01841$
Distance between the coils	$= \cdot02010$
Number of windings	$n = 313$
Diameter of wire	$= \cdot00126$

The value of L derived from the first term of the expression is 437440 metres.

The correction depending on the radius not being infinitely great compared with the section of the coil as found from the second term is −7345 metres.

The correction depending on the diameter of the wire is per unit of length	$\Big\} + \cdot44997$
Correction of eight neighbouring wires.	$+ \cdot0236$
For sixteen wires next to these	$+ \cdot0008$
Correction for variation of current in different parts of section	$- \cdot2500$
Total correction per unit of length	$\cdot22437$
Length	311·236 metres.
Sum of corrections of this kind	70 ,,
Final value of L by calculation	430165 ,,

This value of L was employed in reducing the observations, according to the method explained in the Report of the Committee[*]. The correction depending on L varies as the square of the velocity. The results of sixteen experiments to which this correction had been applied, and in which the velocity varied from 100 revolutions in seventeen seconds to 100 in seventy-seven seconds, were compared by the method of

[*] British Association Reports, 1863, p. 169.

least squares to determine what further correction depending on the square of the velocity should be applied to make the outstanding errors a minimum.

The result of this examination showed that the calculated value of L should be multiplied by 1·0618 to obtain the value of L, which would give the most consistent results.

We have therefore L by calculation . . . . 430165 metres.

Probable value of L by method of least squares 456748   „

Result of rough experiment with the Electric Balance (see § 46)   410000   „

The value of L calculated from the dimensions of the coil is probably much more accurate than either of the other determinations.

Lightning Source UK Ltd.
Milton Keynes UK
UKHW022047180322
400304UK00003B/83